THE LAST HURRAH
The 1970 Tour Down Under

DEDICATION

This book is dedicated to the 607 players who have represented Great Britain, England or Wales in a series or international tournament in the southern hemisphere from 1910 through to 2020.

All of those players have earned the right to be called 'LIONS'

CONTENTS

Acknowledgments

Forward – John Ledger

Introduction

          ****

Chapter One   **Tour Preparations**

Chapter Two   **Queensland Leg of the Tour**

Chapter Three   **The NSW Leg of the Tour**

Chapter Four   **The NZ Leg of the Tour**

Chapter Five   **The Tour Aftermath**

Chapter Six   **The Tour Assessed**

          ****

Personal Tour Recollections

Player Statistics on Tour

Games Played

The 1970 Tour Down Under
ACKNOWLEDGEMENTS

The idea for this book came from a chance conversation with an Australian rugby league fan who had collected a number of the books written on the various tours down under between the two World Wars by the author. I had given a talk at a rugby league forum in Sydney when he approached me. He simply asked if it was my intention to write an account of the 1970 tour to Australia because it was the last time Great Britain had won the Ashes. He also pointed out that 2020 would be the fiftieth anniversary of that tour. Hence the idea was deposited in my mind and this book was born.

As is ever the case in a book such as this there are a great many people who need to be acknowledged for the support and contribution made to the author. First of all, my thanks must go to John Ledger who is the Secretary of the 'Lions Association'. He was so enthusiastic about the book feeling it was long overdue, he readily supplied me with contact details for those players still with us. When I made contact with these players, they enthusiastically supplied me with information regarding their time on the tour. Consequently, my great and heartfelt thanks must go to Tony Fisher, Keith Hepworth, Alan Hardisty, Syd Hynes, Mal Reilly, Jimmy Thompson and Alan Smith for sharing with me and ultimately the reader their personal recollections and insights of the tour. Not only that but they seemed to enjoy being able to bring back into the public domain their exploits in winning those Ashes by talking with the author as much as the author had in speaking to them.

Secondly, the greatest thanks must go to John Coffey author and historian who was a journalist for The Press newspaper in New Zealand during the tour along with other tours he covered during his long career. He readily shared with me his recollections of the tour along with many of the articles he had written at the time. He also wrote his personal recollections of that period and those tourists for inclusion in the book. Thirdly, my thanks go to the noted Australian journalist and rugby league historian Ian Heads who kindly agreed to write a piece covering his own thoughts and recollections of the 1970 tourists and the way in which they played the game. Ian has a long history of covering rugby league and is well respected on both sides of the world.

I would also like to thank Steve Moyse who kindly supplied a photograph of the former Swinton and Wigan player Dave Robinson. Finally, my thanks go to all of the journalists who covered the events of so long ago. Their work in the various publications is recorded by Trove at the National Library of New South Wales and readily available to all via the internet. Without their efforts no record would remain of what happened on the tour both on and off the field. Equally important are the efforts made by all the players, coach and manager of that tour who did what many thought would not be possible. To all those players still with us and those sadly who are no longer I do hope they feel the book does them justice. If I can misquote Julius Caesar "They Came. They Saw. They Conquered."

*(**The Rugby League News** **publication is quoted in this book. The copyright status is undetermined.)**

The 1970 Tour Down Under
FORWARD

FIFTY years. Fifty long years. It is far too many.

Even now, it's difficult to accept that five decades have elapsed since the country that gave the sport to the world last won its most prized trophy: The Rugby League Ashes.

It has not been for the want of trying, of course, for we have come close on several occasions, most notably in the late-80s and early-90s, to knocking the mighty Kangaroos from their pedestal.

But successive national teams have been unable to bridge the gap.

The 50th anniversary of Great Britain's last Ashes success hardly feels like something to be celebrated: There is no glory in coming off second best for half a century.

Yet the exploits of the men who achieved that remarkable feat back in 1970 are most certainly worthy of eulogy and the timing of this terrific book could not be better.

The record of the heroics of the 1970 Lions that are told in the following pages really are the stuff of legend: Of the 24 games they played, the Lions won 22, drew one and lost just one.

Their solitary defeat came in the first Test against Australia, who were subsequently outplayed in the second and third Tests by a group of players who have never been given the full credit their success merits.

Until now.

This book goes a long way to setting the record straight: The term is overly used in sport, but the following pages make it clear beyond any doubt that all 26 players, and their inspirational coach, are true heroes.

Having returned home, the 1970 squad should have been lionised by the governing body, but that did not happen, for reasons that are lost in the mists of time.

The Rugby Football League and its current chief executive Ralph Rimmer, therefore, deserve credit for setting the record straight in 2020 by awarding a specially commissioned medal to the 1970 Great Britain team.

These medals were presented at the RL Lions Association's reunion luncheon in January, an event that has taken place annually since 1946. And we thought those Lions, the Indomitables, were a class act.

Sadly, the long-overdue gesture came too late for too many of the class of '70 with the likes of Roger

Millward, Cliff Watson, Dennis Hartley, Chris Hesketh, Johnny Ward, John Atkinson and Mick Shoebottom having left us.

Time may have taken its toll on the Lions, but the intervening years have provided a glorious perspective to just how special they were and how remarkable their achievement is.

Enjoy the book: let's hope we do not have to wait another 50 years for the sequel.

John Ledger

RL Lions Association Secretary

The 1970 Tour Down Under

INTRODUCTION

It is easy to think given the state of the game of Rugby League in Great Britain today that it has always played second fiddle to the game played in Australia. It is true to say that the Australian authorities that are the NRL have a somewhat arrogant attitude to the game worldwide. To them the game begins and ends in Sydney and their own competition. You will often hear it said by The Australian Board of Control and the NRL that for Australian players the pinnacle of the game is to play Origin football. In other words, to play for New South Wales or Queensland means a player has reached the very top of the sport. That is a demeaning attitude and an insult to the international game.

In truth the NRL clubs dislike international rugby league as they feel that their players should not be placed at risk of injury. To that end the Australian Board now compensates clubs whose players are injured in an international match and forced to miss games for their club. Perhaps closer to the truth is the fact that the income generated from international matches goes into the coffers of the NRL rather than the clubs themselves, hence the reluctance to embrace international football.

Who can forget the furor generated by the Australian Board of Control and the NRL clubs when their players were to play an international game in the United States at Denver, a game between New Zealand and England. Suddenly player welfare was brought to the fore, funnily enough when some of those players returned home and backed up the international match with a club game welfare was not so much of an issue to the clubs. At the end of the 2019 season when Great Britain embarked on a short tour down under the Australians while happy to play Tonga did not want to take to the pitch against the 'Old Enemy'.

That arrogance filters down to the National Rugby League who administer their game with little or no regard to the world game. They year on year seem to alter the rules to suit themselves without going to the trouble of consulting the International Board who are charged with ruling on the game internationally. They have two referees on the field when no other country has. The 2020 season will see the club captain given the option of just where a scrum should take place, the introduction of a 20/40 kick and so on. Each year they alter the rules of the game to suit themselves or more correctly to suit the needs of the television broadcasting companies in their ever-increasing pursuit of more broadcasting revenue. Because of this attitude and approach, it is easy to believe that they have dominated the game since its inception way back in 1895. We tend to forget that the Australian game only came into existence in 1908 some thirteen years after the English game.

The truth of the matter is somewhat different for while the Australians have dominated the Ashes series, such as they are these days, for the last fifty years, that was not always the case. There was a time when the Ashes were in the hands of the English game and were so for around thirty years. The

Ashes which when won in this country way back in 1922 were retained for almost the next thirty years. From the early fifties through until 1970 the Ashes seemed to change hands with a great regularity. From 1970 onwards the Australians began a domination that has remained unbroken up to the present day.

The advent of Super League rugby in 1996 effectively saw the end of the so-called Ashes tours. Tours that were long and involved a three match Test series in both Australia and New Zealand ceased. The reason for this was simply because both hemispheres were to play the game at the same time, in this country we saw the era of summer rugby come to fruition. That as I said was in 1996 and from that time onward the excitement and glamour of being selected to "go on tour" sadly has faded. The present generation of young fans may well have never even heard of 'The Ashes' associating such a term with the game of cricket.

It is then quite ironic that as we celebrate the fiftieth anniversary of the last time this country won the Ashes that the squad that did so was also the most successful touring party ever to leave these shores. When the 1982 and 1986 Australian tourists went undefeated in England and France, they were and still are lauded for their efforts back home. The 1970 Lions are all but forgotten by the game in this country to its shame. They were the fourteenth squad of players that had been selected to tour down under the first squad going down in 1910. It was a tour that had it all, controversy, the despair of a first Test defeat against the old enemy, the joy of winning the next two, to enable them to take the Ashes home for what was to be the very last time. It was a tour which saw the players undefeated in their tour of New Zealand as well.

It was also a tour that was to give to the game some great players the likes of Malcolm Reilly, Phil Lowe, Jimmy Thompson, Chris Hesketh, Tony Fisher, Bob Irving, Roger Millward the list goes on. All of them went on to have great careers and grace the game for a good number of years after the tour. The big question is where did the game go wrong in this country. Following that tour which produced such a wealth of talent why did the game not build on its success why were we to suffer defeat after defeat in Ashes series. Every reader of this book will have their own ideas and opinions but the truth is, go wrong the game did. This book takes us on a journey back in time to that last glorious tour that saw the players prove to be the best ever tour party to represent this great game of ours down under.

The tour saw the whole squad combine to ensure one of them was not served with a writ while up in Queensland an act that perhaps won the Ashes for Great Britain. It saw old battles renewed when Tommy Bishop captained a Sydney Colts side against the tourists. Tommy was certainly not backward about coming forward. Once again, the referees or should that be the referee's interpretation of the rules caused anger and frustration for the tourists. Prior to the vital third Test we saw a country team set out to maim players and put them out of the Test. It was a game where the referee offered little or no protection to the visiting team.

It was a tour that would see twenty four games played in the space of just ten weeks in two different countries. The players literally lived out of suitcases for all that time. If they were not playing, they were training or traveling to the next venue to play. Throw in the need to attend any official functions arranged then you can see just what sort of pressure those players were under once they left Manchester Airport. At the Lions Association annual lunch in January 2020, the RFL presented a special commemorative medal to the players who went on that 1970 tour. Sadly, at the time of writing thirteen of those gladiators of fifty years ago are no longer with us. Many of those remaining are in their seventies and some are not in the best of health. I would suggest that many people in the game today would be hard pushed to remember their names. Perhaps this book will evoke memories once again of who those players were and what they achieved fifty years ago.

The 1970 Tour Down Under
CHAPTER ONE
Tour Preparations

As the 1969-70 season was coming to its close excitement was building amongst players administrators and supporters. The reason for this was quite simple, a tour to Australia was due at the end of the season. Today we seem to have grown used to such matters not being in the rugby league calendar. However back before the advent of Super League and with it, summer rugby every four years the Rugby Football League organized such tours and had done so since the first ground breaking one way back in 1910. To a player being selected for a tour down under was the pinnacle of their career, it was the opportunity to show what they could do in two hemispheres. Also, as the tours only came around once every four years most players only ever got one shot at tour selection hence the high excitement a tour generated.

The season had seen the introduction of two major changes to the rules namely that tactical substitutions after half time were now allowed. From 1964 such substitutions had only been allowed up to half time. Secondly the game of unlimited tackles had been replaced by the four tackle rule. Leeds had continued their domination on the league front topping the table for the fourth season in a row. However, St. Helens led by the great Cliff Watson had turned them over in the Championship final 24-12 with tour skipper Frank Myler winning the Harry Sutherland Trophy as man of the match. In a controversial Challenge Cup final Castleford had defeated Wigan 7-2. Swinton and Hull won the respective county cups and with the domestic affairs settled thoughts turned to trying to win the Ashes back from the Australians.

The 'mythical' Ashes and with them the Ashes Trophy had been sitting down in Sydney since 1963 when the Ashes has been wrested away. Many in the game in England felt that the Great Britain team as they were then, had been robbed of the trophy in the 1966 tour down under. They had fallen not for the first time, foul of some odd refereeing decisions after winning the first Test at the Sydney Cricket ground 17-13. A change of referee by the home authorities who felt that referee Bradley had been too generous to the visitors in their 17-13 win saw them go down 6-4 in a game of numerous penalties and not one try scored up in Brisbane. The third Test was lost also 19-14 again with the same referee Col Pearce in control. To be fair the tourists had contributed to their own down fall on that tour a fact recounted by Cliff Watson much later in his biography.

The tour skipper was Harry Poole who according to Watson was a superb ball playing loose forward who when distributing the ball out wide blew holes in the Australian defenses. The problem was that he did not play in any of the Tests in Australia and the reason according to Watson was due to the Physio Paddy Armour. Poole had a bad knee which would swell up after he trained or played, he kept on telling the selectors he was fit to play but was over ruled by Armour the result was the tourists lost a potent weapon. As Watson recalled when Poole was on the field along with the prop

Brian Edgar the team had two ball players one in the middle of the pitch the other on the fringes and the home sides simply could not handle them. The other quality both players had was that they could play it any way you wanted. If the going got rough neither player was averse to using a bit of knuckle when needed.

When the Australians came in 1967 the series was once again lost by a 2-1 score line but again players felt that the referee Fred Lindop had not had the best of series. True when the first Test had been won in the then graveyard of Aussie touring teams that is Headingley, 16-11, all had seemed rosy. Down at the White City in London the Aussies came back winning 17-11 to level the series. The deciding Test was played in the most atrocious conditions at Station Road Swinton. In truth the home side was out played throughout the game but the first try the Aussies scored by Coote which set them on the road to victory was hotly contested many feeling the player had been grounded short. In the end it mattered little as the game was lost 11-3 and with it the Ashes once again.

Now the aim was to select the players who could restore pride in the English game and with it the Ashes. As was ever the case all had their own ideas as to just which players were capable of doing just that. The newspapers speculated as to which players would be needed to get the job done down under. As ever each journalist had their own ideas with regard to the players that should make the trip. The interesting thing is that down under the Rugby League News in its first issue in January 1970 published an article and it contained the thoughts of Roy Francis the former Leeds coach who was then the coach of North Sydney.

He speculated that there would be a good number of new young players in the squad but it is interesting to look at just who he felt would be in the squad. Of the 'old timers' as he called them, he felt that Bill Burgess, Clive Sullivan and John Atkinson would be named along with Cliff Watson and John Mantle he also felt Bill Ramsey should be in the forwards. He was pretty astute with regard to the newcomers as he named the Castleford trio of Reilly, Lockwood and Dickinson along with Colin Dixon of Salford. In the back he named Syd Hynes and Barry Seabourne. Francis was sure as to who the skipper would be, he was in no doubt it would be Alex Murphy. As we shall see later when Murphy was ruled out of the tour Francis felt the skipper would be the Leeds skipper Seabourne.

Wiser heads than the journalists however, realized that more important than getting player selection right was getting the coach to lead the party right. It was decided that Johnny Whitely the former Hull player and also a tourist himself on the 1958 tour when the Ashes had been won, was the man for the job. That done the selectors sat down to select the twenty six who he would coach. The crazy thing was that as in every other tour that was selected to go down under since 1910 the tour coach was not involved in the selection process.

It was a situation that Johnny Whitely encountered throughout most of his coaching career in the game as he told the author:-

"No, I had no input into who was selected to go on that tour. It was the same when I began my coaching career. Back then players tended to be working class lads, anyone who had a pair of bicycle clips was posh. It was a crazy situation really you would get some bloke who owned a corner shop and he would get elected to the board of a club. He had no understanding of the game yet was having a say in who was selected to play and who was not. It was the same with that tour I saw the names of the players I would coach when the pressmen did. I felt it was unfair that such people were in truth controlling my destiny and my livelihood."

Even before the selectors met to select those who were to go on tour there was controversy. The selection committee was loaded with Yorkshiremen and the criticism was that they would favour players from that county. The second area of controversy was the decision to select only a squad of twenty one players in the initial process. They then intended to select a further five players to make up the full squad two weeks later. The reason for such an approach can only be speculated on as it seems to make little sense. In the early days of tours when players could be away from home for up to four months selectors would approach players and once they agreed to tour their names would be released to the press. It was a drip feed approach that was needed back then but surely not in 1970.

During the second week of March they released the twenty one names to the press and that in itself caused upset. The twenty one players named were:-

Full backs:	Edwards, Price, Dutton
Wingmen:	Atkinson, Smith, Sullivan
Centres:	Hesketh, Hynes, Myler
Stand off:	Shoebottom, Millward
Scrum half:	Seabourne, Hepworth
Loose forward:	Reilly
Second row:	Mantle, Lowe
Props:	Mills, Watson, Ward
Hooker:	Flanagan, Fisher

The Lancashire conspiracy theorists had a field day, Wigan's Eric Ashton expressed incredulity that no Wigan player had been named in the first twenty one. He also felt Price the full back was too slow for international football and was being selected simply for his goal kicking which was a big error. When you look at those players not selected it makes interesting reading. There was no Laughton or Hardisty, no Irving or Thompson. Equally there were only five Lancashire based players in the initial group selected. The Australian rugby league writers were set a conundrum as they tried to assess the players in the squad. They felt the problem area would be in the centre, particularly as Alan Burwell had left the English game for Australia. He had decided to move down under and actually played for Canterbury and many felt he would leave a big hole in the Great Britain three quarter line.

The selection of Syd Hynes as one of the centres set alarm bells ringing with journalists with long memories in Sydney. The reporter for the Rugby League News on the 14 March made the claim of Hynes:-

"Hynes would leave a Duggie Greenall reputation with his uncompromising tackling."

When Greenall had toured down under in 1954, he had been constantly vilified by the Australian press for his style of play particularly during the 1952 tour to England. So angry did he get at the treatment he received from referees that in the last match of that tour he was to walk off the field in disgust! The other thing that was noted by the Australian journalists was that the selectors seemed to be favouring club combinations and they pointed to the five Leeds players selected. The also focused on the Mills and Fisher combination stating the two played together for both Bradford Northern and Wales.

They also were saying that Millward and Hepworth were former team mates before Millward had departed Castleford for Hull K.R. The former Leeds coach Roy Francis now at North Sydney also had his say feeling that when the full squad was to be announced the Leeds scrum half Barry Seabourne would be named captain of the squad. Francis had named him the Leeds captain over Bev Risman when he needed a leader on the field.

The players finally selected by the selection committee and having accepted the invitation to go on the tour, were then released to the media along with the traditional "Pen Pictures" of each individual. These were in parts embellished and printed down under in the Rugby League News on the 18

April 1970. They make interesting reading and show just how far the game has come since those days and also just how little was known of some of those selected. There had been some disappointment down under that Hardisty the Castleford stand off could have missed out having not been in the initial twenty one selected. He had struggled with injury all season but in the Challenge Cup quarter final against Salford he had scored three tries in a 15-0 win. He was running into form and the hope was expressed that he would be one of the players selected for a second tour.

The selectors had been thrown in to confusion when first Mills pulled out of the tour after signing for North Sydney thus ruling himself out of contention. Also, the second row John Mantle had pulled out of the tour for personal reasons. When the selectors met again on the 25 March, they added six new players to the squad. Two young props Stephens from Wigan and Chisnall from Leigh were named. Doug Laughton the Wigan skipper, Jim Thompson the Featherston player, Bob Irving from Oldham and Dave Robinson also from Wigan completed the squad. Just a couple of weeks later, as we know the Wigan prop John Stephens was forced to pull out also. It was then that the Castleford prop Dennis Hartley was named. When they finally got the full twenty six players they wanted the tour party read.

THE LAST HURRAH					The 1970 Tour Down Under

(Photograph published in The Rugby League News 20 June)

(Coach Johnny Whiteley in his playing days)

The Tour Party

Utility Back

Derek Edwards 27; 10.10 Castleford. Plays full back, centre and five-eighth. Toured Australia and New Zealand with the 1968 World Cup team. Substitute in France this season when he played half the game. Welder.

Full-Backs

Terry Price 24; 14-10 Signed by Bradford Northern in 1967. Represented Wales at Rugby Union 1964 to 67 and in Rugby League internationals in 1968-70. Local government officer.

Ray Dutton 24; 13-7 Played for Widnes since 1964. Played for England against Wales and France this season. Driver-salesman.

Wingers

Alan Smith 26;12-9. Played for Leeds since 1962. Represented Yorkshire against Lancashire this season. Played for England against Wales and France in February and March. Cost accounts clerk.

John Atkinson 23; 12-9. Played for Leeds since 1965. Toured Australia and New Zealand with 1968 World Cup team. Played for England against Wales and France 1969-70. Joiner.

Clive Sullivan 27;12-7. Played for Hull since 1961. Member of World Cup team in 1968. Represented Wales in seasons 68/69/70. Miller (Engineering)

Centres

Syd Hynes 26; 12-5. Plays for Leeds. Played against Wales and France this season. Former Leeds and Yorkshire boxing champion. Sheet-metal worker.

Frank Myler 31; 12-4. Tour Captain. Played for Widnes for eleven years and signed for St. Helens in 1967. Has played in seventeen Tests against Australia, New Zealand and France. In the 1960 World Cup team. Toured Australia and New Zealand in 1966. Golf handicap 4. Self-employed.

Chris Hesketh 25; 12-4. Signed for Salford from Wigan in 1968. Played for England against Wales and France this season. Sales representative.

Five-eighth

Mick Shoebottom 25; 12-9. Played for Leeds since 1962. In 1968 World Cup team. Played for Great Britain against France in 1969 and twice for England this season. Is junior champion of Boys Club diving. Welder.

Alan Hardisty 28; 11-0. Played for Castleford for twelve years. Played in eleven Tests against Australia, New Zealand and France. Warehouseman.

Roger Millward

22; 10-5. Signed for Hull K.R. from Castleford in 1966. Played for Great Britain twice against France in 1967/68. In 1968 World Cup team. Electrician.

Half-backs

Barry Seabourne 23; 11-2. Plays for Leeds and has captained them since October 1968. Captained England Under 24s against France and captained England against Wales and France this season. Driver.

Keith Hepworth 28; 10-10. Played for Castleford since 1958. Played for Great Britain against France in 1967. Won first player of the year competition. Races homing pigeons. Wireless mechanic.

Lock Forwards

Malcolm Reilly 22; 14-4. Castleford. Played for England against Wales and France this season. National Coal Board fitter.

Doug Laughton 25; 13-8. Signed by Wigan from St. Helens in 1967. Played for England Under 24 team against France in 1965. Took over captaincy of Wigan from Eric Ashton at beginning of this season. Self-employed heating engineer.

Second Rowers

Jim Thompson 21; 14-2. Signed for Featherstone Rovers in 1966. Played for England under twenty four team against France in 1968/69 and for England against France in 1970. Fitter.

Dave Robinson 25; 14-0. Played for Swinton from 1963 until signing for Wigan in January. Toured Australia and New Zealand in 1966 played in all Tests. Plumber.

Phil Lowe 20;16-4. Signed for Hull K.R. in 1966. Played for England against Wales this season. Apprentice Electrician.

Bob Irving 22; 14-8. Oldham. Represented England against France twice in 1968 and played in three Tests against Australia. Self employed.

Front Rowers

Dave Chisnall 22; 16-0. Played for Leigh since 1967. Labourer.

Cliff Watson 30; 15-8. Played for St. Helens since 1960. In ten Tests against Australia and five against New Zealand. In 1966 and 1968 World Cup teams. Haulage contractor.

John Ward 29; 13-7. Played for Castleford from 1960-70. Recently for Salford, played in six internationals. Publican.

Dennis Hartley 34; 16-6. Transferred from Hunslet to Castleford in 1966. Played for Great Britain against France four times. Motor mechanic.

Hookers

Peter Flanagan (Flash) 29; 12-0. Played for Hull K.R. since 1960. Toured Australia and New Zealand in 1966 and 1968 (World Cup). Represented England against Wales and France this season. Docker.

Tony Fisher 26; 13.6 Signed from Wales by Bradford Northern in 1964. Wales against England and France in all internationals this season. Light heavyweight champion of Far Eastern Forces 1962/64. Driver.

The conspiracy theorists once more had a field day. As there were only seven players from Lancashire in the squad. That number had been bolstered when five for the players named on the 25 March had come from the red rose county. On that same day the selectors named Frank Myler as tour captain and Cliff Watson as the vice captain. There was surprise that the great Alex Murphy had been ruled out of the tour but the journalist Joe Humphreys revealed the reason. Murphy had suffered a bout of flu and a recurrence of a heart infection that was keeping him out of the Leigh team. The selectors did not want to take a chance that he may well be ruled out once in Australia. Ironically down under the Rugby League News in its first issue of the year as mentioned previously had an article in which it was suggesting that Alex Murphy was to be the likely captain for the coming tour.

It was a team that did not suit everyone but there was a great blend of youth and experience in the team. Even some of the younger players such as Irving, Lowe and Reilly had already a great deal of experience under their belts. When you look what was written about some of these younger players by the Australians you realise just how little the Australian press really knew about them. Many in the game felt that the selection of the two Castleford half backs was an inspired choice while others felt they would not be able to reproduce club form at international level. The Wigan Prop John Stephens had originally been selected for the tour but sadly dislocated a hip just before the party were to leave.

As a result, the thirty four year old Dennis Hartley was drafted in. Hartley was just coming off a two match suspension that allowed him to be considered for the tour. Once again in the game many thought the choice a backward step but the coach John Whiteley proved later that it was an inspired choice. He added both grunt and experience into a young set of forwards. Cliff Watson was also elected vice-captain for the tour. It is strange to see that back then the selectors for the tour seemed to have a problem with prop forwards.

One prop considered to be a certainty to tour was big Jim Mills, unfortunately he was persuaded by Roy Francis to sign for the North Sydney club and that decision took him out of contention for the tour. It was a decision he was to bitterly regret by the end of the tour. When you look at the squad the average age was around twenty five and a half years which was not too old or too young for that matter. Generally speaking, whenever a touring side is selected there are always one or two 'bolters' those players who seemed to be picked out of thin air by the selectors so to speak. Players that few if any of the press had on their radar when they were writing who should or should not gain selection.

With this squad there was only one player that could really be placed into that category namely the Leigh prop David Chisnall. He was just twenty two and that was considered to be very young for a prop forward particularly as the scrums were contested at the time. It is a little difficult to put Phil Lowe the baby of the squad into that category as even at his age he had an England cap to his name. So too had the likes of Jim Thompson the Featherstone player at just twenty one, Bob Irving and Mal Reilly at twenty two. Even Dave Robinson at twenty five was selected for his second tour down under and an 'elder statesman' of the pack. These were players who were just making their way in the game in truth. So too were Millward and Seabourne at twenty two and twenty three respectively.

There was experience of the Australian tour conditions in the squad with Hardisty, Watson, Flanagan, Robinson, Edwards and Myler making their second trip down under. In the case of the skipper Frank Myler he had been an international for ten years. If you add to that the fact that Atkinson, Shoebottom and Millward had travelled down under with the 1968 World Cup squad then around a quarter of the squad had been to the place before. Quite a number of that 1968 World Cup squad had not made selection for the tour it seemed it was time for the next generation of players to take centre stage.

It is only when you look closely at the players in the squad that you see just what a great crop of young players the game had produced in this country at that time. With the squad selected there was little time for the media to pick apart the selections as they flew out to Australia on Wednesday 20 May to prepare for the first game of the tour on Friday 22 May 1970 just two days later.

The skipper Frank Myler, told waiting reporters at Manchester Airport before flying out:-

"We have the best possible team and given the time to acclimatise and freedom from injury, we must have a great chance of returning with the Ashes. There are slight differences of rule interpretation in Australia but I think my boys will soon learn to cope."

He and the waiting reporters had no idea just how accurate and prophetic his words were to be.

TOUR CAPTAIN

FRANK MYLER

Frank Myler, of St. Helen's, led his team to a convincing victory over Leeds in the Championship final at Odsal Stadium, Bradford, last Saturday.

Myler, named as a centre in the touring party, can also play five-eighth. He is a stylish mover.

He toured Australia and New Zealand in 1966.

(Photograph from Rugby League News 23 May)

The tour schedule was a punishing one even in the era of air travel with games up and down the two states every two days or so. As ever on such tours, injuries would be the key factor. If the squad remained relatively injury free then they could do well. Should they get a horror run of injuries then possible disaster awaited them.

While the Australian public were excited about the visit of the old enemy it would be true to say that the Sydney media were lukewarm in their coverage not to say underwhelmed in their coverage of the early games up in Queensland. The reason for that was simple. The tour as far as they were concerned was starting the wrong way around. Normally such tours began in earnest at the beginning in Sydney with games against New South Wales followed by the first Test. The tour party then moved off to Queensland a tour of that state and a second Test in Brisbane. This tour was to start in far north

Queensland and then work its way down to Brisbane for the first Test. Sydney journalists were less than happy with the arrangements feeling in some way slighted by those arrangements.

As the date for the arrival of the tourists in Australia got ever closer the publicity was ramped up a little more. There was a quite prophetic piece in the Rugby League News on the 17 May concerning the three Castleford players Hardisty, Hepworth and Reilly. The three were referred to by the writer as the 'back of the scrum trio'. The feeling was that such a combination could spell trouble for the home side in the Test matches. It was what was written by the same reporter of Reilly that catches the eye all these years on:-

"Lock forward Reilly is one of the big 'hopes' of the tour- There are English observers who believe he could repeat the success of the fiery and clever Vince ("Wild Bull") Karalius of the 1958 tour."

Little did he realise just how correct he was in supporting the observations of his English counterparts.

While it was true that many felt the tour was starting the wrong way around, to some extent is suited the Great Britain squad. While it was a fact the opposition in Queensland was not as good as that down in New South Wales the climate and quite punishing schedule the players faced suggested an easier start could be of great assistance. The tourists when the itinerary for the Australian leg of the tour was announced showed they faced a game every two days for some parts of the tour. The itinerary was:-

22 May:	Northern Territories Darwin
24 May:	North Queensland Townsville
26 May:	Central Queensland Rockhampton
28 May:	Wide Bay Gympie
30 May:	Queensland Brisbane
6 June:	Australia Brisbane
7 June:	Toowoomba Toowoomba
10 June:	Brisbane Brisbane
12 June:	New South Wales Sydney
14 June:	Monaro Queanbeyan
20 June:	Australia Sydney
21 June:	Western Division Bathurst
23 June:	Sydney Colts Sydney
27 June:	Newcastle Newcastle
28 June:	Riverina Wagga-Wagga
4 July:	Australia Sydney
5 July:	Southern Division Wollongong
8 July:	Northern XIII Tokoroa
11 July:	New Zealand Auckland
14 July:	Wellington Wellington
19 July:	New Zealand Christchurch

21 July:	West Coast Greymouth
25 July:	New Zealand Auckland
27 July:	Auckland Auckland

It is hard to believe but the tour manager Jack Harding from the Leigh club actually agreed for the team to play an extra game. That game was to be played against a Queanbeyan side on the 14 May and the authorities had actually guaranteed the visitors a gate of $5,000. The Australian rugby league authorities had got their knickers in a twist because the Queanbeyan folks had the audacity to approach the tourists direct rather than going through them. The result was an extra game was allowed but the opposition would be Monaro rather than Queanbeyan. The stupid thing was that the game was actually going to be played in Queanbeyan! The decision does show just how precious the authorities in Australia considered themselves to be at that time.

With the itinerary settled and no last minute injuries from the Championship and Challenge Cup finals to players in the squad the tour could begin. The players and officials flew down to Australia to begin the task of trying to win back the Ashes. They left Manchester Airport on the 20 May and were due to play the first game on the 22 May. They were leaving England and would play the first game of the tour in the tropical far north of the Australian continent. It was a situation that concerned Whiteley greatly as he told the author:-

Generally speaking we would fly into Perth and travel by train over to Sydney. When the tour started you were

playing the big boys of the Australian game. The teams would have international and state players in them and players at the top of their game. You had to be ready to go from day one."

On that tour it started at the top end where the opposition was a lot weaker than down in Sydney. Yet they would then have to play a Test match before travelling down to the far tougher arena that was Sydney. The question was a simple one would the players be battle hardened enough to take on the might of Australia following such an easy lead into the Test. The other thing to remember is that this was the first and only Test series which would be played under the new four tackle rule. Soon after the game changed to the present day six tackle rule.

CHAPTER TWO

Queensland Leg of the Tour

When the players arrived, it was very early in the morning and the temperature was even then in the high thirties. They were greeted in Darwin with the good news that the first game against the Northern Territories was to be played in the evening under lights. The game had originally been scheduled to be played in the afternoon. Given the temperature would be in the high thirties or low forties the English boys were glad. They were to meet a Northern Territories team which was not expected to trouble them over much. The only problem would be the heat and fluid loss during the game.

As the players settled in and started training such as the could the manager Jack Harding from the Leigh club and coach Johnny Whiteley called a team meeting. There a number of issues were discussed and the players made aware of them. The first thing on the agenda was the hard playing pitches that the players would encounter and the need for strapping ankles. They were then told to expect no favours from the referees and touch judges they would come up against on the tours. They were not to get up tight when decisions invariably went against them.

The most important point was made by Whiteley and enforced by Jack Harding. The coach who had toured as a player was able to see things from the players point of view as well as that of a coach. He emphasized the point that on this tour there was to be no Test side and a mid-week side the so called 'ham and eggers'. Right from the first game each and every player was to be given an equal shot at a Test jersey. Players that performed at the top of their game would perform in the Test matches both in Australia and down in New Zealand. It was an issue that raised the spirits of all the players. You get some idea of the problems the coach faced on the tour right from the start;-

"As I said earlier, I had no say in which players were to go on tour I had to work with what the selectors threw at me. I knew I had to get to know each player personally very quickly. I also knew that the players had to get to know each other personally just as quickly. The players knew of each other as the played against each other, that was not the same as getting to know each other. We did not have a lot of time to do that given the programme of matches we had. Equally the players had to get to know the strength of me and what I expected of each and every one of the players. We had around twenty four hours in which to prepare for that first game."

So, it was on a hot, steamy and humid night on the 22 May 1970 the players stepped onto the Richardson Park pitch in Darwin in front of around 3,000 supporters. As expected, the game was no more than a training run for the visitors who ran out easy winners 35-12. It was the sapping heat that prevented an even greater score some of the forwards would lose around four to six pounds in weight during the game. There was little time to digest the game and even to get a proper rehab and training session following the game as the players were required to play in Townsville on the 24 May.

The game was played at the Townsville Sports Reserve and proved a little more taxing than had been anticipated. The game started well enough for the visitors with the forwards quickly making ground down the middle of the pitch. Within a minute of the game starting Phil Lowe stormed in for a try with not a hand laid on him. The two half backs Shoebottom and Seabourne began dictating play and after about eight minutes it was Seabourne who took a pass thirty yards out and sprinted over for the second try. After just ten minutes the score line read 11-0 to the visitors and a huge score looked likely.

It was then that the referee began to penalize the Englishmen and the game would see the penalty count run out to 18-9 in favour of the home side. The visitors scored again and at half time the score was 16-6 with the home side collecting three penalty goals. Early in the second half a penalty try was awarded to the tourists when Seabourne was prevented from scoring and a fifth try saw the visitors leading 23-6. It was then the fight back began the home fullback Moseby was converting penalties kicking seven out of eight attempts. Then the North Queensland side scored two quick tries as the tourists tired to take the final score out to 23-20. It was a wake-up call for the Englishmen.

From Townsville the tour party up sticks bound for Rockhampton and a game against Central Queensland at the Show Ground. The game was won going away as they say by a score of 30-2 and all seemed to be going well. There were few injuries and the players were seeming to 'gel' as a squad. The problem was the easy games were not really preparing the players for what lay ahead in New South Wales in general and Test matches in particular.

THE LAST HURRAH   The 1970 Tour Down Under

(Photograph published in Rugby League News 29 April 1970)

The following day it was announced that an extra game was to be played on the tour. As was mentioned earlier this game had been mooted prior to the players arriving down under.

The Australian Rugby League had taken umbrage against The Queanbeyan rugby league authorities because they had negotiated with the tourists directly instead of the Australian authorities. It was the Rugby League Secretary Bill Fallowfield who persuaded the Aussies to sanction the extra game. He wrote on the advice of Jack Harding that the team was happy to fit in the extra game and so not disappoint the supporters in the Monaro Division. The hosts however in a fit of pique sanctioned the game but rather than a game against Queanbeyan ordered that the team be Monaro District.

As the players travelled to Wide Bay, they were all aware that the first Test was just two games away and in the newspapers the manager Harding and coach Whiteley seemed to reiterate what the players had been told up in Darwin. He told the reporter from The Canberra Times on the 27 May who reported the following day:-

"Every member of the Great Britain Rugby League team is still in with a chance for first Test selection. Performances in the game at Wondai will count just as much for selection as the game against Queensland on Saturday."

The article also highlighted a major problem Whiteley was facing given the hectic scheduling. The reporter told the readers that for only the second time since the team arrived in Australia, they were able to have a training run in the afternoon. The other piece of information was the relatively minor injury list so early in the tour. Utility player Derek Edwards was suffering from a badly blistered foot, Chris

Hesketh had four stitches in a gash on his calf and Mal Reilly was carrying a bruised right knee.

When the two teams took to the field the tourists carried on where they had left off in the last game winning 45-7. The two second rows Robinson and Lowe tore the home defense to shreds out wide while Hardisty and Seabourne ran the whole show. The problem was simply the penalty count against them as the game came to a close, the count was 28-8 in favour of Wide Bay. This group of players were facing the same problems players had faced since the very first tour back in 1910. Those problems stemmed simply from the interpretation of the rules that the Australian referees employed. The referees tended to interpret the rules to suit the local conditions. The problem was a penalty count like that in a Test match would be a disaster and work needed to be done.

It could be said that the tour really was to begin come the Saturday 30 May when Queensland would be the opposition. It was the first real opposition and the players were really under done as they had not really been put under pressure since they arrived in Queensland. The media was looking at the game with great interest as it was felt it would be a test of the mettle of the Englishmen. There was a set back for the team when after a training session Reilly felt soreness in the bruised knee and was forced to pull out of the side. He was not missed as the side put together a good display albeit against a somewhat weakened state side. The game was won 32-7 and so the squad was going into the first Test undefeated. The problem was that they would face an

Australian side containing players they had not yet faced on the field. Also, for the first time they would be walking into that cauldron that was Test football.

The Australian Rugby League not for the first time lost the plot as it were. On the Thursday Jack Harding named a sixteen man squad for the first Test but on the same day the President of the Australian Rugby League Mr. Buckley announced the Test was not to be televised. When pressed by reporters as to what people from the country were to do other than fly up to Brisbane to watch the game live Buckley got a bit shirty.

"I've just told you the facts. It will not be televised you cannot run a tour on nothing."

When he was pressed on the statement about running the tour on nothing he replied:-

"I think it is obvious, if it is on TV for nothing. People will not pay to go and watch the game. The League is not a charitable organization and I am not prepared to discuss it further."

It was not the most tactful statement to make to the media just prior to a Test match. Eventually the game was broadcast on some stations as a delayed telecast with the game being shown at 6.00pm.

There was some concern in the Great Britain camp with regard to the full back position while both Price and Dutton had played reasonably well both were seen to be a bit slow and cumbersome for the Aussie game. It was felt Price would get the nod due to his superior goal kicking ability. Equally problematical was the hooking role. Both hookers had racked up a good number of penalties in the games they had played due to the way referees controlled the contested scrums in Australia. The one area that seemed to be worrying the home side was the scrum with the three Castleford players Hardisty, Hepworth and Reilly selected. The press were of the opinion that having played together for a great number of games at club level if they transferred that form into the Test arena Australia could be in trouble. The truth was that with regard to the scrum half berth Whiteley had little option but to pick Hepworth. The Leeds scrum half Barry Seabourne had torn a muscle in the game leading up to the first Test and was unfit. Little did anyone know at the time but the injury was so bad it would keep him out of contention for the second Test also.

Whiteley had even more pressing concerns as the first Test was coming, as he said:-

"We had gone through Queensland undefeated but the standard of player was totally different to the standard of the English boys. The problem was how do you get through to young players that the Test was a different world. I had a lot of young players who had smashed the opposition, smashed all before them. They had an easy baptism to the game in Australia and I could not get through to them that they were in for a rude awakening.

During the week leading up to the game Arthur Summons who had been appointed the coach of the Australian team named the side that would do battle while Whiteley and Harding decided not to do so until the Friday. As the week progressed the reporters were somewhat critical of the preparations for the game by the Great Britain squad. On the Wednesday the Canberra reporter wrote that the squad, **"Had the quietest Test preparation ever"**. The following day he seemed to be even more critical writing:-

"Yesterday was its last serious training run before the Test and it could not be described as a strenuous workout."

The press perhaps felt that the players were not taking the match as seriously as they should have done.

On Saturday the 6 June the two teams that took to the field were:-

AUSTRALIA

Langlands, King, McDonald, Brass, Cootes, Hawthorne, Smith, Wittenberg, Walters, Morgan, Beetson, Lynch, Coote. Subs Thompson and Weiss.

GREAT BRITAIN

Price, Sullivan, Myler, Shoebottom, Atkinson, Hardisty, Hepworth, Chisnall, Flanagan, Watson, Robinson, Laughton, Reilly. Subs Millward, Irving.

You would have to have a little sympathy with the radio announcers covering the game live. There were just too many Johns in the Aussie line up particularly the three quarter line which was John King, John McDonald, John Brass, and John

Cootes. The other interesting thing was that for the first time in many years the Australian selectors had selected a Test team to play in Queensland and there was not one Queenslander in the starting thirteen.

Given that the visitors had gone through Queensland undefeated many made them favourites for the match. In truth it was a false assumption as they had met with little real opposition certainly, they had not faced a team of Test quality. It showed as soon as the match kicked off with the Aussie forwards taking control. It quickly turned into a real blood and thunder Test match with fist flying here and there. The reporter for the Brisbane newspaper best summed up the opening exchanges:-

"Within ten minutes, Australian second-rower, Ron Lynch, was out of the game with a fractured cheekbone. Artie Beetson was bleeding from the mouth and nose and Jim Morgan's nose had been flattened by a quaintly named, but lethal Liverpool kiss."

In amongst the mayhem the home side kicked three penalties to lead 6-0. In the twenty second minute of the game Flanagan threw out an ill-judged pass which the Aussie prop on debut Morgan latched onto and crashed over for a try. Langlands having a great day with the boot kicked a magnificent conversion and the Aussies had a commanding 11-0 lead. The tourists finally got back into the game when the prop Watson took a pass and surprised the home defense with his speed to crash through for a try by the posts to make the score 11-5.

Sadly, Watson was too badly blot his copybook when in yet another fracas with a number of players milling around throwing punches. Amidst all the mayhem Watson and Morgan squared up and Morgan attempted to head butt Watson but did not make too good a job of it. Watson decided to show him just how it should be done and promptly flattened his nose. The result was an early bath and the visitors forced to play on with twelve men. A drop goal on the stroke of half time made the score 13-5 as the two teams went off for a well earned break.

As the second half began it was important the tourists scored first but it was not to be as the stand-off Hawthorne chipped over the defensive line. The covering Flanagan failed to collect the ball and McDonald picked up the ball and went on to score an unconverted try which seemed to knock the heart out of the Englishmen who were beginning to tire due to the pace the Aussies were playing the game. They were to suffer a little more when shortly after Atkinson stormed away down the touch line from forty yards out to score in the corner. As he got to his feet, he looked back to see the touch judge standing on the line with his flag up claiming the wingman had stepped into touch. The referee wiped off the score.

The Aussies continued to play clinically and in yet another attack the wingman King crossed for a try and Langlands once again added the extras. Great Britain did respond when Flanagan scored a try which Price converted. The home side struck back when Morgan crossed for his second try with Langlands again doing the honours. Hawthorne dropped another goal and the lead was stretched out to 30-10. A couple of minutes later Laughton crossed and Price converted but a penalty from Langlands and a second converted try from King took the final score out to 37-15.

Langlands ended the game with a haul of nine goals and in doing so erased from the scoring record books the great Jim Sullivan for points scored in Tests between the two countries. His seventy seven points were a new record. Also, his nine goals in a game beat the record of Noel Pidding. The tourists had been thoroughly out played in almost every department. Alarm bells were rung by the media. Also, the press really went to town with Cliff Watson calling his actions a disgrace. They were even calling for him to be sent home and not to be allowed to play again in Australia. Morgan for his part told the pressmen that it was him that had started the fracas by trying to head butt Watson, sadly that piece of information did not seem to make most of the newspapers following the game.

It was a ridiculous stance when you consider the mayhem that went on each and every week in the club games in Sydney. There were mass brawls and fighting week in and week out. There were often stand up fights with a number of players involved but all of that was conveniently forgotten by the reporters. They were ever aware of any opportunity to put one over on the Poms. Thankfully clearer heads dealt with the situation, Watson was suspended did his time and then got on with playing the game again. The big problem for the tourists was that Robinson had picked up an injury that turned out to be more serious than first expected. He would not play again during the Australian leg of the tour. It was to be the only really serious injury the tourists were to encounter in Australia.

The press also continued with the autopsy of the game and came to the conclusion that Price as expected had proved to be too slow in the arena that was rugby at the highest level. Also. the hooker Flanagan had not really supplied enough possession from the scrums winning only thirteen to the Aussies twelve. The Sydney press had a field day following the game. After the game they really gave it to the tourists. Some went so far as to write that they were worst team ever to set foot in Australia. The stupid thing was that these same journalists prior to the Test had been predicting that Great Britain would win by at least ten points. You really have to wonder at the stupidity of such writers.

In their analysis, Price was too slow, Flanagan was not the hooker he had been and Watson would prove to be a liability on the tour. They went on to say that Beetson, Wittenberg and Morgan had negated the efforts of the young Chisnall rendering him ineffective. They seem to have forgotten was that the visitors had lost one of the best props in the world at that time in Watson. Finally, they seemed to forget that when the tourists had the ball in hand on attack, they had at times been brilliant and bamboozled the home defence.

Whiteley Recalling that Test stated:-

"There is no doubt that losing Cliff Watson was a massive blow, he was our enforcer. In a game at Test level to lose a player is like losing an arm and Cliff was our pack leader.

I have to say that on that afternoon we were a whimper of a side and were humiliated.

People criticized Terry Price but I would say that he was a magnificent goal kicker his problem was he did not like training. He had come from rugby union where he was looked on as being a super star. He felt he did not need to train. To his credit as the tour progressed, he trained hard we got him fit and his attitude to the game and to the rest of the squad was superb.

As for Dave Chisnall who coped a bit of criticism, I would say that he was one of the young players I talked about who were in the squad. As the tour progressed, he grew immensely as a player and as a man.

I realized after the game that I had a task on my hands. The players had a rude awakening that afternoon. While they could not foresee what happened I surely could. I decided to leave it alone until the meeting we were to have on the Monday."

There is no doubt that the coach and the manager had a big job on their hands if the tour was not to become another disaster. However, the action needed would have to wait until the Monday as Sunday demanded that the tourists take to the field against Toowoomba. In a lack luster performance, the tourists were far too good for the home side scoring nine tries in a 37-13 win. With the game over the coach told the players to get on the 'piss' and let their hair down for the evening. On the Monday morning Whiteley and Harding held a meeting with the players to sort out the situation following the Test loss.

"I sat all of the players down on that Monday morning and the first thing I said to them was to reiterate that as far as I was concerned there was to be no more talk of "Ham and Eggers" we were a squad of twenty six. When I had toured, I was lucky enough to be in the so called Test side but there was no doubt in my mind that such actions split the squad into two groups. I was determined it would not happen on this tour.

You can believe me or not but I tell you this I had mapped out in my mind every single training session I intended to run while in Australia. I told the players that if they were prepared to train as hard as I wanted them to do, they would win the Ashes. If they did that they could do what they liked afterwards. I then got the players to have their say.

I will tell you something else about that tour that I am proud of and it is simply that each and every one of those players on the tour arrived back home with a Test cap to their name. They either played against Australia or against New Zealand. I don't know if it has ever happened before or since. The other thing that pleased me that when we got back home every player was fit enough to go out and play for their club."

The skipper Frank Myler said following the game that the team was going to have to tighten up on its tackling if they were to get back on track. Much later in an interview he was of the opinion that the first Test really ensured that the Ashes would be won. He said that all Tests are intense as they should be however, on that afternoon up in Brisbane the tourists came of age. The got their backsides kicked and got a good hiding but they realized that day just what was required of them if they were to win a Test series against the Australians.

As was to be expected the players were really down following the defeat and none more so than Watson the vice-captain who felt he had let the team down by getting sent off. The players were not used to losing and had gone into the game expecting to win. They also knew they were up against it as the referees and touch judges were really not giving them an even break. At the meeting some of the younger players vowed they were not going to take a backward step for the rest of the tour. They were going to give the Australian teams as good as they got. Watson also stood up and told the rest he was going to lead from the front and felt they really could beat the Aussies.

He was supported by Dennis Hartley the tough as teak prop who vowed there was to be no surrender on the field again. Players such as Mal Reilly, Phil Lowe, Jim Thompson and Doug Laughton stated they were prepared to follow Watson's lead and if the Aussies wanted it rough then that was what they would get. There would be no moaning about the referees but rather they would play on despite decisions that went against them. Whiteley and Harding also worked very hard that week encouraging the players and telling them they had the beating of the hosts and the Ashes were not yet lost.

They had an early opportunity to prove to themselves and the media that had written them off that they were very much alive. On the Wednesday they were to play Brisbane at the Exhibition Ground. As they were preparing for the game the manager Jack Harding was thinking ahead. He was aware that the team was to play Monaro down in Queanbeyan south of the capital Canberra in the week of the vital second Test. He asked the Australian Rugby League for permission to remain in Queanbeyan after the game returning to Sydney on the Friday just prior to the Test match. His argument was that the cooler climate would help the players during training. In truth he and the coach were probably well aware of the spotlight the players would be under from the press in Sydney.

The manager Jack Harding following the Test at Brisbane had a nice little catch up with two Australians who had played for Leigh in the past. One was Trevor Allan who was commentating on the game for the A.B.C in Brisbane. The other quite incredibly was Mick Bolewski who had signed for the Leigh club following the 1908-09 tour by Australia to England on the ill-fated Giltinan tour. Bolewski was eighty one years old when he met up with Harding!

On the Wednesday the final game in Queensland was to be played They went out that day with a little more steel and resolve in their play following Whiteley's team talk. There were a number of changes to the team with Hardisty selected to play on one wing and Smith on the other. Derek Edwards was to play at fullback as he had at Toowoomba. Hynes and Hesketh would be in the centre and Seabourne and Millward at half back. Sadly the second row Robinson had damaged an ankle in the Test as was out of contention for selection for the game and would be side lined for a few weeks. The tour was well and truly placed back on track as they blew Brisbane off the park winning 28-7. Roger Millward stood up that day and with two tries and five goals for a personal tally of sixteen points gave a statement of intent for the second Test.

At this point it may well be worthwhile to look at the travel the players had to undertake while they were in Queensland. From the first game up in Darwin until the final game in Brisbane. They played in Darwin on the 22 May and the last game in Brisbane was on the 10 June. In total that was just nineteen days during which time they played eight games but travelled around 4,200 kilometers or in old money almost 3000 miles, it was a punishing schedule by any standard. However, little did anyone know at the time as the squad prepared to pack up and fly down to Sydney there was far more serious trouble on the horizon and it would break as the players were due to fly to Sydney and then to Queanbeyan.

It is inevitable when you have young players away from home that trouble will follow them around and so it proved to be the case as the trip to Queensland was coming to its conclusion. Whiteley takes up the story:-

"Some of the players were at a party and there was a guy there who worked for one of the airlines. He began calling young Reilly a 'Pommie Bastard' which was not really a good idea. Unfortunately, he continued in the same vein and Mal had had enough and promptly head butted him.

The guy then took out a writ for assault against Mal and all hell broke out in the newspapers. It was headline news up in Brisbane and not only the back pages but the front pages as well.

Following the last game against Brisbane we were actually on board the airplane ready to fly to Sydney when there was an announcement over the intercom asking if a Mr Malcolm Reilly would please identify himself by pressing his attendant buzzer. It was hilarious as all had an idea what was happening when a young lady was seen in the aisle at the front of the plane carrying an envelope. I think everyone on board pressed their button. The girl quickly realized that she was not going to be able to identify Mal and serve him with a writ."

The Canberra Times on the 11 June carried a small piece that showed just what was happening:-

"A Supreme Court writ was issued in Brisbane today against Malcolm John Reilly a member of the Great Britain Rugby League touring team. The writ issued by John Ryan, of Oates Parade, Northgate, Brisbane, claims unspecified damages for alleged assault. No particulars were disclosed."

Ryan claimed that he had been attacked and hospitalized and was claiming $60,000 in damages, hence the writ being issued. Reilly's problems began before the players boarded the aircraft and it was Dennis Hartley that averted the danger. As the players were walking to the airplane, he saw a young lady and a man approaching with writ in hand and realized what was about to happen. He got the players to surround Reilly and walked him onto the aircraft before the pair could get anywhere near him. Once on board as Whiteley recalled with now the young lady standing writ in hand at the front of the aircraft an announcement was made. Reilly was asked to identify himself by pressing his call button. All the players pressed their call buttons. Not only that but many of the other passengers did the same.

It was vitally important that the writ was not served on Reilly for if it had due to the crazy laws in Australia, he would have not been allowed to leave the state of Queensland. We tend to think of Australia as one country and that may be true but all the states have different laws. In order to get Reilly to return to Queensland from New South Wales then Queensland would need to apply to extradite him back! As it was, he was able to continue on the tour until such time as the Queensland authorities gained permission from the southern state to serve Reilly with the writ.

The Canberra Times on 12 June carried an article that laid out the comedy of errors that was the attempts to serve the writ on Reilly. The firm charged with serving the writ sent three representatives to the airport in an attempt to identify Mal. They mingled with the players armed with newspaper photographs of the player. One of the servers told reporters they had been trying for twenty four hours to find the player and he believed that he had spoken to Reilly without knowing just who he was. One wonders if the incompetence of the writ server that day lost the Ashes for Australia. Would the tourists have won the last two Tests if Reilly had not been in the side?

When the aircraft took off and left Queensland the players were preparing to get ready for the second and toughest leg of the tour. They were on their way to New South Wales in general and Sydney in particular. They had ground to make up being one down in the series and just over a week or so to go until the now crucial second Test match came around. The trials of Mal Reilly were left behind in Queensland for the time being at least. They would though not go away.

CHAPTER THREE

The NSW leg of the Tour

The tour party was to make their way down from Sydney to Queanbeyan to the south of the Australian Capital Canberra. Harding and Whiteley as was stated earlier wanted to remain in the town following the game against Monaro. By doing so the players could get down to some serious training with a good recovery time between each session. Also, they would be out of the spotlight and the plan was to travel up to Sydney on the Friday as the game against Australia was to be played on the Saturday. Sadly, news arrived that the Australian Rugby League would not allow that to happen. Strange as it may seem they had arranged a Civic Reception for the tourists on the Tuesday and needed the squad back in Sydney on the Monday.

The game against Monaro was scheduled to be played on the Sunday and the Aussies wanted the tourists back in Sydney on the following day. In the initial stages the officials down in Monaro were quite angry as the Australian Board had given no indication why they wanted the squad back in Sydney on the Monday. It was thought the Board had a fit of pique over earlier run ins with the Queanbeyan authorities. It was only with some reluctance they issued a statement regarding the Civic Reception for the players planned for the Tuesday.

Before that the players were to face New South Wales at the Sydney Cricket Ground on Saturday the 13 June. All eyes were on the game as many felt the whole tour rested on both the result and performance of the visitors. Many felt that if NSW were to win then the second Test was a foregone conclusion as was the series. The players were under no illusion as to what they faced that Saturday afternoon but no one had any idea of the renewed vigor and steel that the coach and the manager had managed to instilled into each and every player.

One of the criticisms the newspaper men made of the players was that they were not fit enough. This rankled Whiteley who was and still is a fitness fanatic. He decided to knock this criticism on the head and out of the minds of the players while preparing for the NSW game:-

"I had asked the players to increase the intensity of our training. But I also told them, why should an Aussie player be fitter than you simply because he runs on the sand at Bondi Beach in the sunshine. You people trained by running along the banks of the Humber in the depths of winter. You ran up and down the Pennines again in the depth of winter. Training in those conditions gave you all an inner strength a core strength as good as if not better than what an Aussie gets from running on the sand in the sunshine. The lads took it on board and did everything I threw at them in training for the rest of the tour."

The players certainly responded to the call to train even harder. Mal Reilly told the author:-

"**The coach used to knock me up around 6.00am. before training to go for a run. By the end of the tour nearly all of the squad were voluntarily getting up and joining us.**"

The reporter from the Canberra Times on the 13 June gave a hint as to what New South Wales and the rest of Australia could expect from the Great Britain pack for the rest of the tour when he wrote:-

"**England have been instructed to move up fast and knock the NSW players over before they can run. Forward leader Cliff Watson has been given the task of showing his players the method and it will be up to the others to follow suit.**"

There was little doubt the right man for the job had emerged as Watson said later in his biography. His view was the Aussies did not like it if you got up into their face. You had to play with a lot of mongrel and knock them down if they had the ball or not. You never let them run or they would tan your hide. Get into their faces. For the rest of the tour that is just what everyone of the players were prepared to do.

Knowing just how important the game was to the rest of the tour a very strong side was selected:-

Edwards, Sullivan, Myler, Hynes, Atkinson, Millward, Hepworth, Watson, Fisher, Hartley, Thompson, Lowe Laughton. Subs. Shoebottom, Ward.

Opposing them was a strong NSW team consisting of:-

Langlands, Grimmond, Cootes, McDonald, King, Lye, Smith, O'Reilly Walters, O'Neill, Costello, Thompson, Coote. Subs Rhodes, Thompson.

In the Great Britain lineup that afternoon in the pack was the youngest tourist in the squad in Phil Lowe and the oldest in Dennis Hartley. With Hartley and Fisher along with Watson in the front row coach Whiteley was to say later that it was the last time Great Britain had a world class front three. The game however did not start well for the tourists.

In the first half the game turned into a forward battle typical of a Test match really which many of the press felt it was. It was New South Wales that were to go into the dressing rooms at half time leading 6-2. Langlands had slotted over three penalties to Roger Millward's one. Things got decidedly worse as the second half got under way. Prop O'Neill managed to break the defensive line and slip the ball to Coote. He raced away and then fed the wingman King who scored the first try of the game.

With the score line reading 15-2 to the home side following a field goal and penalties the tourists were stung into action. As they had done in the first Test up in Brisbane as the second half progressed, they began to take control of the game. They were to score three tries through Atkinson, Hynes and Doug Laughton all converted by Millward. Then a sixth penalty by Langlands had tied the game at 17-17. The visitors could and should have won the game but a try saving tackle by the centre John Cootes late in the game denied them a victory they deserved. The increased training seemed to have done the job Whiteley desired. In the second half the NSW hooker Walters was injured and had to leave the field and there was a doubt about him being fit for the upcoming Test.

The game although not won caused a bit of a stir amongst the press reporters who quickly stopped all talk of a home whitewash and began hinting that Australia had a hard job on their hands if the Great Britain team continued to show the sort of form they had at the Cricket Ground. The game over the squad prepared to depart for Queanbeyan and the game the following day against Monaro. As they did so they were to see the Australian Rugby League had added just a little spice to the up coming game the tourists faced against a Sydney Colts side.

It was the Rugby League News that broke the story that an exception was to be made to the Sydney Colts side in as much as the English scrum half now the captain coach at Cronulla Tommy Bishop had been invited to captain the side. The game due to be played on Tuesday 23 June at Endeavour Field Woolooware had been arranged to celebrate the bi-centenary of James Cook landing on Australian soil for the first time at Kurnell. The Kurnell site at Botany Bay was quite close to the Cronulla club's ground and is referred to as Captain Cook country.

On the Sunday 14 June the tourists took on a Monaro side and as expected proved to be too strong for the home side. They won the game easily by a score of 34-11 but paid a heavy price for the victory when they lost full back Ray Dutton with a dislocated shoulder. The injury reduced the options

Whiteley had at full back in the Test match the following Saturday. The other worry was the heavy penalty count of 24-5 in favour of Monaro the referee imposed on the visitors. A penalty count like that in the Test would see the Ashes in all probability staying at home in Sydney. Smith the wingman scored a hat trick while Hardisty, Hesketh, Thompson and Irving also had big games to remind the selector that they were wanting a Test jersey.

On the Monday the squad returned to Sydney and began training at the home of the South Sydney club. There was one particular feature of their training ground which pleased Whiteley if not all the players:-

"At the training pitch there was a man-made hill and after training I got every player to run up and around that hill six times. I myself did it so there was no complaining from the players. I have to say that Dennis Hartley and Cliff Watson benefitted greatly from that extra training."

Cliff much later in his biography said of this extra session that when the tour was under way all thought that Dennis Hartley was going to be third in line behind himself and Dave Chisnall. It never bothered Dennis who simply got on with doing his work. Johnny knew Dennis was not fit enough and needed to shed a little weight for the Aussie games so he and I went up that bloody hill a great many times I can tell you. We called the thing 'Pork Chop Hill.'

On the Tuesday the Australians named the team for the second Test and there were a number of changes. The prop

Morgan had not recovered from the broken nose he received curtesy of Cliff Watson in the first Test. The second row from that first match Lynch had also not recovered from injury. The hooker Walters had injured his chest in a club game and so he was out and while Langlands had been named as full back and captain there was a doubt about him. He had injured a thumb in the club game on the weekend and it would later prove to be broken and so he would be out of the side. The tourists for their part decided to keep their powder dry and only name their team on the Friday.

In the end the manager Jack Harding relented and on the Wednesday, announced the team to play in the vital second Test. There were seven changes from the Brisbane game. Derek Edwards who had played very well against New South Wales on the weekend replaced Price at full back. Alan Smith who had run into a rich vein of form replaced Clive Sullivan on the wing. The fast improving Syd Hynes replaced Mike Shoebottom in the centre and Millward replaced Alan Hardisty. In the pack Dave Robinson was injured while Flanagan and Chisnall were replaced by Fisher and Hartley both of whom had played well on the weekend. Reilly had recovered from a bruised hip and played while the tough tackling Jim Thompson would take Robinson's spot in the second row.

True to their word following the first Test loss Harding and Whiteley had selected a team that was the best available to them on the form shown on the field. Those players that were playing well got the Test jerseys for the game. Manager Jack

Harding also it seems indulged in a bit of mind games of his own. He spoke with reporters and informed them:-

"I am delighted that Langlands has been replaced by Laird at full back. We have played against him twice on our northern tour and he continued to kick to us. Our problem has been winning the ball but with Laird at full back we will probably see more of it."

Laird was in the habit of coming into the attacking line and chipping the ball over the approaching defenders. It was a tactic Whiteley had noted and worked out what to do to defend against it. In the lead up to this vital Test match all was going very well for the Great Britain squad, too well.

The following day the news broke that Malcolm Reilly was in hot water yet again. He already was dodging a writ being served on him from up in Brisbane. It would appear that Reilly on the previous Saturday morning the day of the New South Wales game had been asked to leave the South Sydney Leagues club. A South Sydney player Kevin Longbottom reported that he had been involved in a fight with Reilly outside the Leagues club. The matter had been brought to the attention of the manager Jack Harding. He in turn had obtained the facts and then after speaking with Reilly had sent a report back home to the English Rugby League Council.

The Council decided they were too far away from the situation to act so very wisely contacted Harding and left the matter in his hands. They informed him to do whatever he deemed appropriate. Harding discussed the matter with

Whiteley, the skipper Myler and vice-captain Watson. All were of the opinion that Reilly was too important to the cause to be sent home early. His decision was to fine Reilly $160 and that was to close the matter. He was not so stupid as to play into the hands of the Aussies and suspend him from the upcoming game. Reilly writing later in his own biography made the important point that it seems it is fine for Australians to abuse the Pommies and call them whatever names they like. However, it is not alright for the Pommies to retaliate in any way. It was however a distraction the squad could have done without. Whiteley much later was to say to the author:-

"Reilly was quite a handful but he was inspirational as a player and a trainer. He had such courage and strength that belied his stature and was so enthusiastic about the game. He was a phenomenal trainer and on the tour if I went for a run he would always accompany me."

It is easy to see just why Harding and Whiteley wanted Reilly playing in the Test rather than sitting in the stand.

The two teams for the vital second encounter were:-

AUSTRALIA

Laird, King, McDonald, Brass, Cootes, Hawthorne, Smith, Wittenberg, Fitzsimmons, Sattler, Coote, Beetson, Weiss. Subs Fulton, Costello.

GREAT BRITAIN

Edwards, Smith, Hynes, Myler. Atkinson, Millward, Hepworth, Hartley, Fisher, Watson, Laughton, Thompson, Reilly. Subs Shoebottom, Irving.

It was a warm sunny day ideal for playing rugby league that greeted the two teams as they took to the field. A huge crowd of 60,962 cheered to the rafters especially the Australian supporters who were expecting to see their team clinch the Ashes. Sadly, it became obvious right from the start they were to be bitterly disappointed. The home side appeared lack luster and lifeless when faced with a strong tough defense from the tourists They often say "cometh the hour cometh the man" and the British certainly had the man that afternoon his name was Roger Millward. He tore the Australians to pieces first with his individual brilliance but also with his disciplined team play something Whiteley seemed to have instilled in each and every one of his players that afternoon. What was important was that first they played for each other if they did that the individual skill factors would kick in.

The game was only three minutes old when Reilly put up a huge 'bomb' Laird failed to get to it in time and made the classic mistake of letting a rugby ball bounce. Who was there to capitalize on the error but Millward who collected the ball and was over for a try before the Australians realized just what had happened. He then rubbed salt into the wound by tacking on the extra two. Just a few minutes later he kicked a superb forty yard penalty to stretch the lead. In the twelfth minute from all of thirty yards out he let fly with a drop goal that sailed sweetly between the posts to make the score line 9-0 much to the annoyance of the huge crowd on the famous 'Hill' who were getting more and more raucous and fractious.

The rattled home side tried to get back into the game but were constantly repulsed by resolute and uncompromising defense particularly from the British forwards. Thompson and Laughton knocked down all that came at them out wide. Hartley Fisher and Watson had the middle of the park completely sewn up as well. Reilly, well Reilly was Reilly that game here there and everywhere on attack and especially on defense. The only score the Aussies could manage in that first half was a McDonald penalty. That score was cancelled out soon after by that man Millward and when the players left the field for the half time break the score read 11-2. What was needed from Great Britain was another forty minutes of the same and the Ashes series would be still alive.

He still got ball away

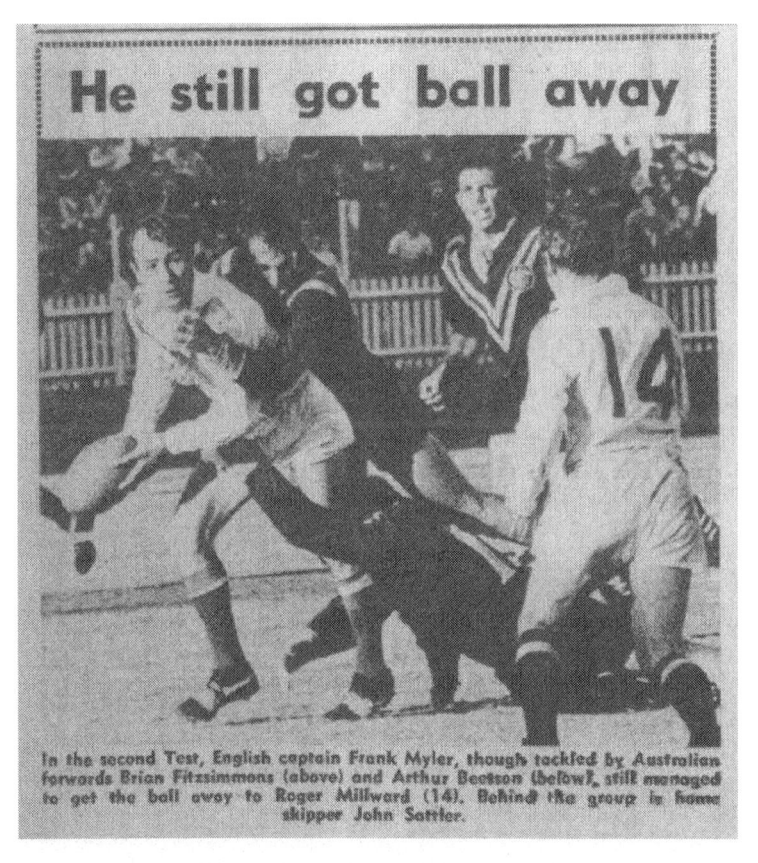

In the second Test, English captain Frank Myler, though tackled by Australian forwards Brian Fitzsimmons (above) and Arthur Beetson (below), still managed to get the ball away to Roger Millward (14). Behind the group is home skipper John Sattler.

(Photograph published in The Rugby League News 4 July)

As was to be expected as the second half commenced the green and gold players exerted great pressure but the defense of the visitors continued to hold firm. Both McDonald and Cootes failed with attempted penalties. As is the case after soaking up all the Australian pressure it was the British who scored when in the fifty third minute the Leeds centre Syd Hynes coolly dropped a goal and the score line read 13-2.

Sadly just a few minutes later he was to blot his copybook big style. He was on the receiving end of a late tackle to the head from the Aussie second row Artie Beetson. Or to be more precise Beetson's elbow smacked Hynes flush on the side of the jaw dislodging a couple of teeth in the process. Typical of Hynes he took exception and it seems he aimed a kick at the offending Beetson while he was lying on the ground but missed or Beetson got out of the way.

The touch judge was on the field with the speed of an Olympic sprinter waving his flag like a whirling dervish. The report to referee Don Lancashire was that Hynes was guilty of attempting to kick Beetson! Lancashire called Hynes over to him and Hynes protested his innocence claiming he had missed in his attempt to kick Beetson. To the dismay of the British players and Hynes Lancashire pointed to the dressing room. It was the second blow the team had suffered in just a short time. A couple of minutes earlier the full back Edwards had been badly injured and forced off the field to be replaced by Shoebottom.

If the home team and the crowd thought this was to be the start of a revival that would see Australia go on and win the game, they were sadly disappointed. They did manage a drop goal of their own from Hawthorne a couple of minutes after Hynes departed. The truth was that it was the tourists who proceeded to take the game by the scruff of the neck once again. Though a man down they simply blew the Aussies away running in three tries in the process. The first try seemed just retribution as Beetson who was not having the best of afternoons failed to collect a rolling ball. The winger

Atkinson strolled in picked up and went in for a try converted by Millward and the score read 18-4. With around five minutes left Roger the Dodger struck again and collected his second try of the game. It was then that something resembling farce took over.

The hooker Tony Fisher who was hobbling on one leg with a knee injury and simply making a nuisance of himself in defense had his moment of glory. The Australians desperately trying to get out of their own twenty five yard area threw out a 'Hail Mary' pass. The hobbling Fisher intercepted and needed only one good leg to run the twenty five yards to the line and score without a hand being laid on him. It was a score that seemed to be the last straw for the home supporters for it sent the crowd into uproar. With Millward converting the two tries he took his personal haul for the game to twenty thus equaling the record of Lewis Jones back in 1954 and Langlands in 1963 as record point scorers in a Test match between the two countries.

With the game won the tourists took their foot off the gas and this allowed the winger King to score a consolation try in the seventy eighth minute to make the final score 28-7. When the final whistle blew that signaled great celebrations on the field from the red white and blue shirted players. It also signaled a mass brawl amongst the supporters on the 'Hill'. Pitched battles raged and the police in attendance struggled to restore order. It is unclear if the trouble was caused by too much ale being consumed or the disappointment of supporters at the inept performance of their team.

Most likely it was a combination of both. Certainly, the try scored by Fisher seemed to have sent sections of the crowd on the 'Hill' into fits of rage aimed at the ineptitude of their own players. Cliff Watson would recall later that the press who had made such a fuss of his sending off up in Brisbane remained strangely silent about the crowd violence that afternoon. The other thing they were quiet about was just how well the tourists had played that afternoon and that they had not allowed the home side to play at all. Strange people Australian rugby league writers! The bottom line was that as the players left the field that afternoon the series was now tied at one game each.

The players celebrated as did the coach and manager at a job well done but the tour was not over, far from it, a trip to Bathurst awaited the players. The opposition was to be Western District and the game was to be played the following day. It was a little bit of an anti-climax as the players could not really let their hair down following their win. It is though interesting to get an Australian perspective on the Test match and we can do so by reading what was written in the Rugby League News following the Test under the headline;-

"BRITON'S SUPERIOR TEAMWORK PREVAILS

Great Britain through superior team play and the individual brilliance of the little five-eight Roger Millward convincingly won the second Test at the Sydney Cricket Ground last Saturday 28-7.

Thus, they completely reversed the result of the first Test in Brisbane and ensured that the third Test in Sydney next Saturday would decide the rubber.

The British camp fielded a reorganized and stronger team; Australia suffered from the absence of full back Greame Langlands, hooker Elwyn Walters and Prop Jim Morgan through injuries. Langlands was seriously missed because of his playing skill, his goal kicking and his fierce competitive spirit.

However, the fact is that Great Britain had achieved striking improvement through profiting from lessons in Brisbane and from their determination to keep in the contest for the Ashes. Great Britain won the Sydney match with a highly impressive all-round effort. Their defense especially forward had improved; their attacking play functioned strongly where as in Brisbane it had only fluttered. And there was Roger Millward to keep darting here and there worrying the Australian scattered defense.

On the other hand, Australia's defense was far less reliable than in Brisbane, here and there through lack of speed. There was a lack of cohesion around the scrum; The makeshift goal kicking failed.

Great Britain led 11-2 at half time. When centre Syd Hynes was sent off the field by referee Lancashire on the report of a touch judge after eighteen minutes of the second half (to be charged with attempted kicking and a severe caution) Britain led 13-2.

A few minutes earlier, they had to replace plucky lightweight full back Derek Edwards who was injured Mick Shoebottom coming on. But there was no sustained Australian rally indeed the tourists hit back with three tries. The last try was shattering to the huge crowd; Hooker Tony Fisher who was limping from a knee injury, gathered in a loose Australian pass and loped twenty five yards to the goal line."

It was a well balanced piece and stated just what had occurred in the Test and was welcomed by the players. There were many reasons for the increased performance from the Great Britain team but undoubtedly the main one was that the coach Whiteley had managed to get through to them just how tough they would need to be and how well they would need to perform if they were to win. The easy games up in Queensland had led to a false sense of security in the players. Perhaps a feeling that they were so much better than the opposition that they could not lose. The first Test had shocked them but Whiteley had picked them up and instilled a new belief and a better understanding of what the players needed to do. I think as well "Pork Chop Hill" may well have played a part also. Now though the third and final Test was looming up and it really was a game that needed to be won if the tour was to be deemed a success.

Of course, the inevitable conspiracy theorists appeared out of the woodwork claiming as was ever the case that the home side had thrown the game. The reason being that by going to the final Test with the series tied a good gate was assured. The media was in no doubt the Australians had not thrown the game they had simply been out played by a much better side on the day. They did make such comments with more than a little reluctance and tempered them with the fact that four players from the first encounter were out injured. They were however, also very worried now that with the momentum firmly in the Great Britain camp the Ashes could be going back to the 'Old Dart'.

As had been the case through out the tour a big game was followed with a country game the next day. This time as was stated the players faced a trek out to Bathurst to meet Western Division. The players really did have little time to celebrate or let their hair down. It was a game they won going away by a score of 40-11. The problem was that there were no easy games and effort was needed but players were not being given time to let their body repair itself or relax following big wins. On the return to Sydney it was then the turn of Sydney Colts to face the tourists.

While out in Bathurst for the game the coach Whiteley had a nice little catch up with three of the players who had been with him on the 1958 tour when they English had won the Ashes. It was a tour long remembered simply because the skipper Alan Prescott had played most of a Test match with a broken arm and had refused to come off. With the game at Bathurst over Whiteley met up with Dave Bolton the former Wigan stand off who was now plying his trade with Balmain. Dick Huddart who was the player coach at Dubbo Macquaries made the trip to the ground as did Phil Jackson the former Barrow tourists. Jackson was running a pub at

Narromine at the time. It was a nice break for the coach from the duties of trying to win the Ashes back,

When you think of a Colts side you think of young players just making their way in the game. The series was tied at one all and the Aussie selectors were not going to give the visitors an easy ride particularly in Sydney. They selected a very strong side led by the little fire brand that was Tommy Bishop to face the touring party. The game was the Australian rugby league world's tribute to Captain James Cook who had set foot in Australia for the first time some two hundred years earlier.

There were almost 15,000 at the ground when the teams took to the field and the play was to put it bluntly somewhat rough. Worrying for the visitors was the fact that Millward was forced off the field after just ten minutes with a slight groin strain. The manager and coach were taking no chances with their star stand-off. In typical fashion one or two of the Englishmen had a bit of a dig at Bishop who responded in kind much to the delight and amusement of the supporters watching. In the end the game went the way of the tourists by a score of 26-7. Equally concerning for the visitors was once again the number of times the hooker Flanagan was penalized at the scrum. It seems he went through his whole repertoire of offences possible in the set scrums, foot up and loose arm seemed the most popular. The problem was that the referee Keith Holman was a former Australian scrum half so knew all the dodges hookers got up to.

The players did get some free time and Cliff Watson related in his biography an incident when he and Dennis Hartley along with other players went to get a massage and then went on to get a haircut. The hairdresser told Dennis he should get a toupee he reckoned it would take years off him. We all talked him into getting the toupee and the hairdresser fitted it. The result was amazing as he looked ten years younger. We went back to the hotel for dinner and no one noticed the hair piece, Dennis was made up. The following morning Watson got a phone call from Hartley who was in a bit of a state as he could not refit the toupee. We all tried but we could not get the thing back on properly. In the end we gave up, stuffed the thing into a paper bag, went back to the hairdresser and Dennis got his money back.

On the Saturday the squad travelled up north of Sydney to the coal city of Newcastle. It was a fixture that had become a tradition having been played on all the previous tours. Sadly, the city was no longer the power house it had been and the game was won with ease by a score of 49-16. On the Sunday the players had to travel down from Newcastle to Wagga-Wagga where they were to face a Riverina side. The fixture was the last the tourist would have before the final Test. There is little doubt that they had been set up in that game.

The Riverina team were to be coached for the game by none other than Arthur Summons who just happened to be the Australian national coach and would be preparing the Aussie side for the final Test come Saturday. It is unclear if the Riverina officials appointed Summons or the Australian Rugby League did. Summons was based in Wagga Wagga the town the game was to be played at so it could well have been the Australian Board that made the decision. It became obvious very early on just what the tactics were to be that Summons had instilled into the team. It may well be better to let the reporter for the Canberra Times best describe what went on that afternoon:-

"Great Britain received a big surprise and was lucky to score a one point win over Riverina at Wagga today.

After leading 5-4 at half time it trailed 11-7 half way through the second half but was saved by an intercept try by John Atkinson. Price's conversion gave it a 12-11 win.

Great Britain did not have a happy day against a hard tackling Riverina side. From the first tackle Riverina forwards led by John Hobby and Brian McPherson made the Englishmen feel as though they were playing in a Test.

There was a punch in almost every tackle as Canberra referee Bruce Chapman issued many cautions but no one was sent off. England suffered four casualties and used three replacement during the game.

An ambulance was taken onto the field to take full back Derek Edwards to Wagga hospital. He was later allowed to leave suffering from a badly bruised thigh and he returned to Sydney on crutches tonight.

Winger Alan Smith has a fractured thumb, captain Frank Myler stiches in his head and half back Keith Hepworth a swollen hand. Edwards was injured when he was crash tackled by Riverina hooker Wayne Linsell as he

attempted to field a kick near his own line. The ball rolled loose. Hobby diving on it for the try which gave them an 11-7 lead.

Ten minutes later English hooker Flanagan intercepted and when caught by the defense on the right hand touch line cross kicked to Atkinson on the other side of the ground who toed the ball through and fell on it to score.

Great Britain has lost only one match on the tour, the first Test and today was the closest it has come to a defeat by a country side.

Much of the credit for Riverina's good performance must go to Australia's coach Arthur Summons, who planned the tactics which almost brought off the biggest rugby league upset in many years."

It is pretty easy to see just what those tactics were from Summons just six days out from the third Test. There is little doubt the opposition were intent on doing as much damage to the Englishmen as was possible in the hope of 'softening them up' for the Test match or even putting them out of the side. It really was a disgraceful exhibition from the home side. Coach Whiteley was in no doubt either just what was happening that afternoon:-

"There was absolutely no doubt what the tactics were and what Summons who was the Aussie coach at the time wanted. It was a vile game and the opposition just went out to maim our players. It was brutal and we got no protection from the referee that afternoon. Edwards was crash tackled without the ball and badly injured. The problem is that when you are in that kind of game your skill factor suffers you are too busy protecting yourself. We came through it and managed to scrape a win.

I know what the intention was by the Australian players and coach for that matter but it actually worked against the Aussies and into our favour. I told all the players that we had been in a brutal game and won. If we can withstand that sort of brutality and lack of protection from the referee then we can withstand whatever brutality is thrown at us in the Test. I also told the lads that if that was the only last chance strategy the Aussies could come up with to win, if we play as we could play, we would win the Test and we would win the Ashes."

On that Monday the Australian selectors released to the newspapers the team that would play in the third Test at the Cricket Ground. They had made seven changes from the team humiliated in the second Test. It was an all New South Wales team and yet another full back was being played. McKean while a good attacking full back was suspect in his defense and that suited the Englishmen. In the centre was a player making his debut who would go on to become the scourge of future Great Britain teams in the form of Bobby Fulton. It was however, the front row that interested coach Whiteley, Beetson, Walters and Morgan had been named and Whiteley had no doubts that his front three had the measure of them.

The coach made his feelings known to reporters when the Australian team was published:-

I believe the switching of Beetson to the front row could backfire. Beetson is a marvelous player but he is not a front-rower his mobility in the loose will be lost by this move."

Not for the first time on the tour the English coach was spot on with his comments. For the second time the home selectors had made seven changes to their side for the final Test. Such moves never auger well for success at this high level.

As the week progressed sadly preparations were somewhat disrupted for the tourists on two fronts. On the Saturday the news had broke that the South Sydney club had been in negotiations with the Leeds player Mick Shoebottom and agreed terms with the player. This in turn had brought a quick response from the Leeds club in the form of Jack Myerscough;-

"They say they will now negotiate with us but they have picked the wrong club for a start. We are not interested. We just don't want to know. And I would like to make that clear to them before they begin.

In England it is illegal to approach a player before speaking to his club. Over there they tend to negotiate with the player and then go to his club."

The article went on to quote Shoebottom saying that if the Leeds club did not agree to the transfer he would emigrate to Australia. However the last word on the whole affair went to Jack Myerscough;-

"If anyone emigrates from our club they will emigrate out of the game."

(The transfer never transpired and Shoebottom returned and played for Leeds during the 1971-72 season. Sadly, while playing for the club against Salford in the Championship semi-final he was badly injured. Shoebottom while scoring a try was sadly kicked in the head accidentally by Colin Dixon. He was carried from the field unconscious and for a time the medical people were very concerned as for a while he was paralyzed. He did make a slow and difficult recovery from the injury but never played the game again.)

In truth it was a distraction but was not going to over trouble the preparations for the Test something far more serious could well have done so. Coach John Whiteley related the events;-

"We had finished training and were going back to the Olympic for lunch. As I walked into the place there was a chap sitting at the bottom of the stairs and he asked me who was the boss. When I told him, I was the coach and so one of the bosses he told me he had a writ to serve on a Malcolm John Reilly and would not be leaving until he had done so.

I found Jack Harding and we decided that it was best to get Mal to accept the writ which he did. We were then faced with getting legal representation for Mal. We had a bank account into which the players paid. It was money they got for advertising stuff or appearing at functions and so on. All the players agreed we should use the cash in the account to get legal help for Malcolm which we did. The daft thing was that once we got ourselves a solicitor to keep Mal out of the hands of the law the whole affair simply died a death and we never heard anything further. I think that whole thing helped the players as they felt all were against them and they were not going to buckle whatever pressure was placed on them."

The say the wheels of justice turn ever so slowly but turn they do. Once the writ was served on Reilly the law took its course and the matter appeared before the court When it did the players all rallied round Reilly, they set up a fighting fund and each of the players chipped in £35 to pay the legal costs. Reilly was though free to play in the vital third Test.

On the Thursday of that week Whiteley recalled exactly when he felt sure that the team would win the upcoming Test on the Saturday;-

"We were all sat in the Olympic having lunch after a training session and I was sitting with Jack Harding chatting. Suddenly there was a clatter and crash of a knife and fork on the plate. I looked up and heard Dennis Hartley call out 'I feel bloody marvelous' I turned to Jack and told him there and then we were going to win on Saturday. I could sense that Dennis was simply saying what all of the players felt. We were ready for the Aussies."

As they had done all the tour Harding and Whiteley on the Wednesday released a sixteen man squad to the newspapers.

Alan Hardisty was added to the squad and Terry Price recalled to cover for the injured Edwards. Harding was quite adamant that he would not release the team to take to the field until the morning of the Test which irked the pressmen greatly. Come the Thursday plans were in a bit of disarray when Terry Price was confined to bed suffering from influenza. Also, he was having heat treatment on a back injury. Whiteley when questioned about Price told the waiting reporters;-

"I ordered him to stay in bed and we are giving him ray treatment and antibiotics.'

He went on to say that he hoped that Price would be fit to play at the weekend but he would know more after training on Friday. Ominously he told the press;-

"The worry over Price was the only disappointing feature of todays training. It was the best session we have had in Australia and Price or no Price I think we will win on Saturday.

The forwards have worked a treat, the halves have never gone faster and the outside backs moved quickly and handled safely."

There was no doubt that Price's condition was a worry for the coach as both Edwards and Dutton the other full backs were injured and unable to play. Mind you he did have an ace up his sleeve in Mick Shoebottom who had come on for the injured Edwards in the second encounter and played very well at the back. While both coaches and sides were confidant of winning the Ashes there was no doubt that Summons was the more worried. The newspapers revealed he had been spending a good deal of time promoting team confidence. Whiteley had no such worries.

On the Friday Terry Price did not train but the Aussies curtailed their training early, Summons stating he was happy with preparations. He did identify the same area that Whiteley had done when he told reporters that for his money the front row was the most important spot in the team and the team that won that contest would sew the match up. They were words that turned out to be very prophetic. Harding on the other hand kept his cards close to his chest stating that Price had until 11.00am on Saturday morning to prove his fitness.

If we are to believe the newspaper reports then it would appear the home side were lacking a little in confidence. The reporters were writing that Summons the coach was seeking to instill confidence in his players by having daily team talks. There is no doubt the mood in the Aussie camp was much more subdued than it had been following the first Test win up in Brisbane. They say the bookmakers rarely get it wrong in these situations and they had Great Britain at 2/1 on and Australia at 2/1 against! That was a fact that would have worried the home side and its supporters greatly.

On a perfect afternoon for rugby league there were 61,258 supporters crammed into the Cricket ground to greet the two teams that were to do battle. The two teams lined up thus.

AUSTRALIA

McKean. McDonald, Fulton, Brass, King, Hawthorne Grant, Morgan, Walters, Beetson, McCarthy, Costello, Coote. Subs. Lye, Weiss.

GREAT BRITAIN

Shoebottom, Smith, Hynes, Myler, Atkinson, Millward, Hepworth, Hartley, Fisher, Watson, Laughton, Thompson, Reilly. Subs Hardisty, Irving.

Price had not recovered sufficiently to play and Shoebottom was called up. Smith played with his thumb strapped and Hepworth a bandaged hand. If the second Test had been won easily by the Great Britain side the final Test was even more comprehensive in spite of the close score line.

As the match began it was obvious that the referee Don Lancashire was intent on exercising control of what was a tinder box situation. In the first ten minutes he almost blew the pea out of the whistle and the result was a lead of 6-2 to the green and gold. McKean slotted over three penalty goals to one by Millward all for off side or scrum offences as both teams were over eager. The situation changed drastically in the twelfth minute of the game. Following up from a kick through by the visitors the Aussie full back McKean collected the ball and attempted to get a clearance kick away from his own twenty five yard area. Dennis Hartley came galloping in and charged down the kick.

He kicked the ball on and a kind bounce allowed him to pick up and he crashed over the line with the Aussie second row Costello hanging on to him. Millward had an easy kick to take the lead at 7-6 for his team, it was a lead they were destined never to relinquish. In all probability that one piece of action by the Castleford prop would have pleased Whitley more than any other on the tour. Hartley was in truth the third choice prop and many had criticized the selection, the coach knew that he would bring a great deal of experience to the pack. It was experience that was greatly needed when you look just how young the back three were in that Test side.

The Great Britain boys were well in control of the game at this point and built up the pressure to such an extend that after just twenty minutes they would score again. Beetson who like he had in the second Test was not having the best of times threw out a wild overhead pass. Atkinson ever alert intercepted the ball and ran away to score in the corner without a hand being laid on him. Just a couple of minutes later they were in again and it was set up by Reilly. He had been a thorn in the side of the Aussies since the game had started and once more he took on the defensive line. On this occasion he put in a beautifully weighted grubber kick and it led to the ever alert Syd Hynes crossed for the three points. Millward tacked on the extra two and the score was 15-6.

All the Australians had to show was two further penalty goals from McKean and incredibly they were still within range of the tourists in spite of never seriously challenging the oppositions try line. At the half time break it was still 15-10 to the visitors. Ten minutes into the second half McKean stepped up once again to slot over a glorious penalty from all of forty five yards out making the score 15-12. It did not take the Englishmen long to respond and it was Shoebottom the makeshift full back who did the damage. He ran at the defensive line with purpose and strength and they could not hold him. Having got through he went for the try line when he looked like being tackled, he dummied to pass inside, waited, and sure enough the ever present team mate of his Atkinson appeared on his outside shoulder. Atkinson took his pass and scooted over for his second try which Millward failed to convert to make the score 18-12.

With twenty minutes of the game remaining there was yet another twist in the tale. Watson who had been driving the ball up time after time and knocking Beetson back on his arse as he did so took the ball up one more time. Beetson who was having the proverbial nightmare and seeing himself and his team being out played let his frustrations get the better of him. As Watson was being tackled Beetson came in and let fly with a hay maker smacking Watson on the head. To his credit the referee Lancashire showed his true mettle when calling Beetson over and pointing to the dressing room. The crowd went wild as they knew with his departure any chance of winning the game went with him. Beetson really should have known what was to happen as the referee had already cautioned him along with about half a dozen other players from both sides.

In truth as Whiteley had predicted before the game by switching Beetson to the front row it had negated his ball playing abilities and frustrated the player himself. It was

Beetson's pass in the first half while he was in the mid field that had led to Atkinson crossing for a three pointer. As the game had gone on Beetson had got more and more frustrated. I suppose Watson charging at him one more time it was the straw that broke the camel's back.

Yet another penalty from McKean once again closed the gap to 18-14 and then the crowd in the ground went berserk. A chance kick through from the home side prop Jim Morgan saw them scramble the most unlikely of tries when McCarthy fell on the ball over the try line to make the score 18-17. In truth the scorer McCarthy was well in front of the kicker Morgan when he scored and the try should have been disallowed for off side. It was a point a number of the players strenuously made to the referee to no avail. It was just another strange decision by Lancashire that favoured the green and gold that afternoon. As McKean stepped up to attempt the conversion from the touch line you could have heard a pin drop. It was a cruel situation for the tourists to be in four minutes from the end of the game. They had totally dominated proceedings from the kick off but were now in danger of losing the lead with the clock ticking down. Thankfully the kick sailed past the outside of the right hand post and justice was served. With the score reading 18-17 the visitors could not afford to rest on their laurels as the game was coming to its close.

THE LAST HURRAH   The 1970 Tour Down Under

Watson holds the Ashes trophy aloft after Great Britain had beaten Australia in the deciding third Test at the S.C.G. in 1970.

(Vice-Captain Watson parades the trophy around the Sydney Cricket ground)

The Great Britain boys though had not finished and they conjured up a fifth and final try that sealed the game and the Ashes. With the game almost at an end Reilly slipped out a peach of a pass to the supporting Laughton who crashed through the defensive line once he got his arms free and was in the clear he carried on the move by looking for support. The ever alert Millward appeared at his side and took the pass forty yards out and sprinted round the cover defenders to score a try going away. He failed to convert the try but by then no one really cared the Ashes were back in English hands. The final score line failed to do justice to the dominance the Great Britain team had exerted over the Aussies. Five tries to one tells its own story.

It has to be said the referee Don Lancashire made a number of shall we say strange decisions during the game which resulted in the home side keeping in contact with the opposition via the penalties McLean converted. Certainly, footage of the try the home side scored shows clearly the scorer was well off side but the try was given. To his credit however, he did not hesitate in sending Beetson from the field much as he had done with Syd Hynes in the second Test. It was also clear that the words of Australian coach Arthur Summons had been correct in as much as whoever won the front row battle would win the game. The Great Britain coach Whiteley would say later;-

"The front row of Watson, Fisher and Hartley were magnificent in that game. Dennis Hartley was a replacement in the squad when Stephens had to pull out injured. He grew in stature as the tour progressed, he got better game after game. He relished the whole thing the glory of winning. He did everything I asked of him and he put his hand up to play if we were stuck be it a Saturday or mid-week game.

He and Watson in my opinion in those last two Tests were the last time we had a world class front row. With Fisher

in the middle they would have taken on any front row the Aussies or anyone else had and beat them."

In his biography much later Cliff Watson revealed that the domination of the opposition front row had begun at the very first scrum. Watson had broken Jim Morgan's nose in the first Test causing him to miss the second encounter. As the first scrum was forming up Watson called out to Morgan, "How is the nose doing Jim?" Morgan did not respond and as Watson said "If someone had said that to me, I would have smacked them on the nose straight away. Jim never reacted and I knew then he was not going to trouble us."

Watson was as shocked as anyone when Beetson got his marching orders but knew why he had done what he did;-

"I have been getting up Beetson's nose all the game and when I ran up at him again, he let fly with a haymaker which caught me on the head. In truth it was not his style really he was not that sort of player but I think he was very frustrated not just because we were out playing the Aussies but because he was having a shocker."

The odd thing is that in the white hot atmosphere on and off the field that afternoon Johnny Whiteley remained as cool as a cucumber;-

"As I sat and watched the game, I could see the level of commitment and skill from my lads and I just had a smile on my face. There was no way we could lose that game the attitude of all the players was superb, they had bought into what I had been saying to them since we left

Queensland. The front three as I said were magnificent but also you had to ask the question just where did Jim Thompson come from? His tackling was ferocious and he battled for every yard of ground he had made. He went from nowhere to a star that game. With him going forward like that it made Doug Laughton and Mal Reilly have a platform to use all the skills they had. Add to that the work little Roger Millward did darting here and there and how Frank Myler kept everybody going and their mind focused on the job what else could I do but sit back with a smile on my face and watch.

I will tell you just how good those lads were that afternoon even the Australian press acclaimed them and that does not happen too often. The wrote of the discipline of the squad and the way they had entertained the public in every game. They also felt we had played Test football as it should be played that day. I have never been prouder as a coach than I was that afternoon. Even the Australian supporters in the ground stayed and applauded the Great Britain players that afternoon. That is how well the boys played that day."

(Featherstone Rovers Jim Thompson in his tour jersey)

There were one or two in that vast crowd that had mixed feeling as the players did their lap of honour. One of them was big Jim Mills who said of his feelings that afternoon.

"I was actually selected for the tour but I made the worst decision of my entire career. I let Roy Francis talk me into signing for the North Sydney club. I went to all the three Tests as a supporter. I think the incident between Cliff Watson and Jim Morgan was instrumental in us winning the Ashes. I will tell you why because what Cliff did was to show the Aussie forwards that there would be no backing down by the lads. If they wanted it rough then boy, they were going to get it rough. When the final whistle went at the end of the third Test, I have never felt so lonely in my life. I watched them carry the trophy round the field and I could have been on that field with them. I do have to say that on that afternoon Watson, Fisher and Hartley were just brilliant."

(The fearsome threesome that caused so much trouble to the opposition Hartley, Fisher, Watson)

Sadly, as had been the case all through the tour the players could not really let their hair down and celebrate. The reason was that on the following day the tourists were to meet Southern Districts down in Wollongong. The players could have been forgiven for not really being interested in the nondescript and seemingly meaningless game. After all they had accomplished what they had set out to do which was win back the Ashes so they could relax now. That was an attitude that Whitley had eliminated from this squad of players. They went out and once again produced a winning performance walking off the field 24-11 winners. They had not lost a game since the first Test and the only blot on the record was a 17-17 draw with New South Wales.

On the Saturday evening following the Test win there was one last official function to be carried out in Sydney. Jack Harding and the squad went to the City Tattersall's Club for a farewell dinner where they were presented with the Ashes Trophy.

This was a trophy that had first been presented back in 1928 at the instigation of James Giltinan. He had persuaded the City Tattersall's Club to present a trophy to the side that won the series in Australia versus England clashes. This cup typical of the Rugby League had a somewhat checkered history. The trophy had for a time been lost back in England. It was last seen at a dance organized by the Aussie 1933-34 touring party and had gone missing. The Aussies claimed they had handed the trophy to the hotel manager, he in turn claimed never to have received it.

It was missing for a good number of years only to be discovered in a cupboard at the hotel the dance had been held at in Illkly in 1945. The hotel had changed hands and the cup was discovered when a full inventory was made of the building and all the rooms and cupboards were searched. That was back in the day when for thirty years it had been the English game that had dominated world rugby league. Luckily in the years it was missing the English won each of the series. When it was actually re-discovered there was great relief simply because in the 1950 series it was the Aussies who were to reclaim the Ashes. They had not done so since the 1922 series when they had toured this country.

THE LAST HURRAH								The 1970 Tour Down Under

*(The cup was first presented in 1928 and is inscribed
International Rugby League Australia v England (The Ashes)
Presented by the City Tattersalls Club 1928)*

THE LAST HURRAH   The 1970 Tour Down Under

> July 11, 12, 1970   RUGBY LEAGUE NEWS   Seven
>
> **City Tatts' Trophy Presented**
>
> At the farewell to the British party at the S.C.G. last Saturday evening, team manager Mr. John Harding (left) shakes hands with the chairman of City Tattersalls Club, Mr. Laurie Taylor, after Mr. Taylor had presented the "Ashes" Cup.
> City Tatts' trophy will remain with the English League at least until the next Kangaroo tour. Others in the picture are: The Premier, Mr. Askin (extreme left), deputy-chairman of the Australian Rugby League, Mr. Norman Robinson (centre), and Messrs. Charles Bannerman (asst.-secretary of N.S.W. League) and John O'Toole (A.R.L. member), right.

(The Rugby League News 11 July shows the Ashes Trophy being hand to Jack Harding)

Normally with the Australian leg of a tour over, there was a tendency to say the job had been done and the New Zealand leg was a sort of holiday jaunt. Whiteley and the players were having none of that. On the Tuesday they flew down to the Dominion to start the Kiwi leg of the tour and were determined to carry on where they had left off in Sydney. Sadly, only twenty five of the players got onto the aircraft.

The back injury that Price was suffering from had not responded to treatment and in fact was beginning to worry Whiteley and Harding as well as the player. The decision was taken that Price would enter the Royal North Shore Hospital for specialist treatment. Such was the problem that Price would remain in hospital throughout the New Zealand leg of the tour. He only rejoined the squad on its return to Sydney to continue flying home.

As had been the case through out this tour there was little or no time to relax or even prepare for games. The players flew from Sydney on the Monday and were to play the first game of the tour on the Wednesday. I shudder to think what the present day players would make of such a schedule, player welfare would surely preclude it from happening these days. The issue for the coach was a simple one just how much hard training was required of the players for the last nineteen days of the tour. During the Australian leg Whiteley had maintained the precise level of fitness needed without causing players to 'burn out'. That was one of the outstanding features of his coaching skill on the tour. Could he maintain that balance while in the Dominion.

CHAPTER FOUR

The New Zealand leg of the Tour

Once the game in Wollongong had been completed the players had to prepare for the flight to Auckland. That was on the 6 July and they were to play the first game of the New Zealand leg of the tour on the 8 July. As had been the case in Australia there was not a lot of time to prepare. The squad was required to play a three match Test series against the hosts as well as four provincial games some on North Island and some on South Island. Once they had settled into Auckland the team that was to play a Northern XIII was selected and on the 8 July boarded a bus to make the 200 kilometre or so journey south to Tokoroa for the game.

There is no doubt that Whiteley was aware of the pit falls facing touring parties moving from Australia to New Zealand. Players were fatigued and carrying niggling little injuries for a start but the conditions in the Dominion carried their own difficulties. Players had to adapt quickly from the bone hard pitches they had encountered in Australia to the heavy waterlogged pitches that were the norm at this time of year in New Zealand. Equally difficult was to reacclimatise from the heat in Australia to the winter like conditions of England that also was the norm.

Whiteley felt that the move to New Zealand actually rejuvenated the team:-

"It all stemmed from the training regime we had put in place. I had quickly learned just what each player could give me. We also were playing on some quality pitches and it was refreshing to the players to get tackled and

actually sink into the ground rather than bounce off it as they had in Australia. That one thing worked in our favour.

With the first Test coming up quickly I was not worried as the whole squad had a winning temperament. People may say we were lucky with injury but I do not think that was the case. Because we had a squad of twenty six and used all of them we had spread the work load and so players had remained fit whether that was luck or good management is up to others to say."

It must also be said that history tended to favour the home side as every touring side that had triumphed in Australia, the 1946, 1958 and 1962 squads all had lost the first Test in New Zealand. In fact, to add weight to this belief it had been thirty four years and six previous tours since the last winning 'double' had occurred. What was needed from the tourists was the same steel and determination that they had displayed in Australia if the were to win the three match Test series in New Zealand.

When the players arrived, the newspapers were full of speculation as to who would be selected to face Great Britain. The press was full of reports that Roger Bailey the talented but contentious stand-off would gain the unenviable job of facing Roger Millward. The former Wigan ace Cecil Mountford had been appointed manager of the Test squad and the coach was to be a Wellington man, Morris Church who would look after the playing side of the team. There was one bit of disappointing news that greeted the players and that was the announcement from the authorities that the Test matches would not be televised live. The offer the authorities had received from the New Zealand Broadcasting Corporation was considered to be inadequate. Given the struggle the game faced back then from the rugby union game it was a crazy decision in truth. Surely national exposure of the Tests would have allowed the public to judge for themselves the relative merits of the two codes.

The Great Britain players would have been aware of the weight of history that was on their shoulders as they prepared for the first game of the tour. Certainly, the manager and coach were as they selected nine of the players that had won the third Test in Sydney to play at Tokoroa. There was still a problem with the full back position and Myler was selected to fill that role. Hynes was carrying an ankle injury but was expected to be fit to play. Whiteley would be able to see how his players had travelled and who was ready for the first Test. Equally importantly in the Northern XIII were a number of players expected to play for New Zealand in that Test. The coach would get his first look at some of the opposition.

The game proved to be tough but only in the first forty minutes when the score was 13-12 to the visitors. They had been down 0-7 early in the game but had worked their way back into the match as was to be expected on an energy sapping heavy ground it took them a while to get it together but when they did, they trampled over the opposition. The star of the game was undoubtedly Syd Hynes with two tries and six goals for a personal haul of eighteen points. He was closely followed by the Featherstone find of the tour Jimmy Thompson who while scoring two tries himself paved the way for several others by his blockbusting runs. Further tries by Atkinson, Flanagan, Hesketh, Hardisty and Lowe took the score out to 42-17 at the close. The only worry was once again the very high penalty count against the tourists as had been the case in Australia.

In an attempt to combat this Harding and Whiteley had a meeting with New Zealand officials to discuss the interpretation of the rules the home officials were employing. It seems that it was just that, talks, as the penalties continued to come thick and fast their way in the future games. With the first Test next on the agenda it was the home side that had problems. When they selected the team, they opted for Bernie Lowther to occupy one of the centre berths. Lowther the youngster had gone from club to international in the space of less than two months. He had excited home officials with his attacking play in a game against a New South Wales country side earlier in the season and on that basis was to face Frank Myler and Syd Hynes. There are baptisms of fire and baptisms of fire!

The other thing was that reporters felt that the duel between Roger Bailey and Roger Millward could be the key to victory. Whiteley was in no doubt it would be the front row battle once again that would decide the outcome. In a quite bizarre twist just prior to the game the New Zealand coach Church told reporters that he had a secret weapon that would win the game for the home side. Sadly, he refused to reveal just what it was. Given the form the tourists had shown he would have needed to give each of his players a stun gun if they were to win.

The other problem came due to an influenza epidemic that was sweeping the country. Dixon a second row had been selected for the Test but had gone down with the flu. His replacement was to be Ron Hibbs the problem was that he could not be contacted. A phone call from officials to his family in Greymouth informed them that Hibbs was working out in the bush twenty miles or so out of Greymouth. While his mother packed a bag for him his brother, a policeman, set out to locate his brother. When Hibbs arrived home, he picked up his bag and raced to the airport where a ticket to Auckland was waiting.

The only injury worry for the tourists concerned the scrum half Keith Hepworth who had injured his arm in the final Test in Sydney. X-rays showed there was no bones broken and the player was expected to play but if he was unfit then Seabourne would take his place. Whiteley told the waiting reporters when the team for the first Test was announced:-

"The team knows just what is required of them. It is not our intention to be like other Ashes winning sides and come unstuck in the first Test in New Zealand."

Whiteley would reveal much later that he had a motivational tool up his sleeve that he was to use whenever he felt the need during the tour:-

"I used to say to the players that they would never be as good as the 1958 tourists *(Whiteley had been in that squad that had also won the Ashes)* **It became a bit of a thing with the players. When ever they came off the field having won, I would face a barrage from them and their cry was always the same 'Whack that Whiteley'. I never got tired of hearing them shout it either I can tell you."**

The other thing to consider is that all through the tour the work load had been spread. There was no player that was asked to play when not really fit. Equally important was the good luck, the tourists did not suffer any horrendous injury problems. While it was true that Price had been left in a Sydney hospital Whiteley felt the injury was more due to simple wear and tear than a specific rugby injury.

"When we played the Sydney Colts side up in Sydney Price played full back and I can tell you he was in magnificent shape and form. He was outstanding in that game I always felt that he could have been a real super star in our game if he kept himself in the right shape and got his mind set right. The back problem was an on-going thing, I think rather than being due to an injury sustained on the tour"

On the Saturday of the Test Hepworth was declared unfit to play and Seabourne stepped into fill the void. The two teams that stepped out at Carlaw Park on that Saturday to contest the first Test were.

NEW ZEALAND

Ladner, Orchard, Christian, Lowther, Brereton, Bailey, Patrick, Orchard, O'Neil, Gailey, Hibbs, Deacon, Kriletich.

GREAT BRITAIN

Shoebottom, Atkinson, Myler, Hynes, Smith, Millward, Seabourne, Watson, Fisher, Hartley, Thompson, Laughton, Reilly.

When the game kicked off it did not take long for the visitors to get on the wrong side of the referee who was already racking up the penalties mainly for scrum offences but also because the Englishmen were off side at the play the ball. Sadly, for New Zealand the ace goal kicker Ladner was to have an off day but did kick two penalties to give his side a 4-0 lead. It was then not for the first time Millward showed his individual brilliance and opportunism when the ball went loose on the home twenty five yard line. Quick as a flash Millward kicked the ball through and following up touched down for the first try of the game.

Just a few minutes later Watson was instrumental in the next try scored by Laughton. He burst through and drew Ladner the full back and passed the ball to the supporting second row forward. Further tries followed from Hynes and then Atkinson just before half time to take the tourists score out to 14. They were now in complete control and really should have been out of sight unfortunately the home side were kept in touch by the referee who penalized the tourist with almost monotonous regularity. If they were not encroaching within the five yards at the play the ball, then they were not tackling correctly. At the scrum you could take your pick foot up, not a straight feed it mattered not the whistle blew. As the half came to an end the score read 10-14 to the tourists as Ladner converted field goals and penalties.

The visitors while on top could not generate any consistent play due to the constant holdups in the game. As the second half got under way it was the Kiwis that were to strike first. A loose pass was picked off by the stand off Bailey who then fed his wingman Orchard who crossed for a try that Ladner could not convert. The crowd sensed a victory in the offing with the score now at 13-14. Syd Hynes stretched the lead to 13-16 when he in turn kicked a field goal. The ground was taking its toll on both sided and a forward battle developed. The strong bursts from the likes of Watson, straight up the middle of the pitch, Laughton doing the same but out wide on either flank were the order of the day. Inevitably it was Reilly that had the crowd on its feet with his footballing efforts.

Fisher had the crowd on its feet also but for a different reason. He was pulled out and cautioned by the referee following his tackle on the scrum half Patrick. It transpired Fisher caught the scrum half with a stiff arm which resulted in the Kiwi being stretchered from the field and replaced by Walker. The defense of the tourists was as strong and uncompromising as ever it had been. But they struggled to add points as was said due to the plethora of penalties they were conceding. With the game still really in the balance because of that fact it was the brilliant Millward that was to settle the matter.

With just over ten minutes of the game remaining Millward took a pass at speed and when he hit the defensive line accelerated even further to go clear. With the cover defense coming across and closing on him and it seemed he was going to be tackled by Christian and the move halted he put in a cross kick. His judgement was spot on and the ball bounced in the centre of the field perfectly for Laughton. The second row collected the ball and sped in at the corner for his second try and took the score out to 13-19. A last minute penalty goal by Ladner completed the scoring and the first Test was won by 15-19.

The Kiwi Full back Ladner a renowned goal kicker had managed to convert only four penalties from eleven attempts and this had contributed to the defeat in many respects. His two field goals had helped keep the side in touch with the tourists but it really was the referee that had been the catalyst for a poor score line from the Englishmen. He awarded eighteen penalties to the home side and this contributed to Fisher losing the scrums twelve to nine so starving his side of possession somewhat. It was the penalty count that worried coach Whiteley the most and this after discussions with the authorities aimed at reaching a consensus as to how the rules were going to be interpreted.

In spite of all of this the particular banana skin that was the first Test had been avoided and the winning record was still intact. However, the issue of the penalty count had to be addressed and it seemed that talking to the New Zealand authorities had clearly had little effect. The question was simple had the authorities communicated with the relevant referees or had the referees simply ignored the information and refereed as they always did. Whichever it was the players needed to come up with some way of combating the penalty count against them.

With the Test match won it was time for the players to travel to the very south coast of North Island for a game against a Wellington Invitation XIII. On the injury front there was good and bad news for the squad. The bad news was that both Seabourne and Hepworth were unfit to play both carrying minor injuries and so Millward was to be pressed into service at scrum half as a replacement. The good news was that Dave Robinson who had been injured in the first Test up in Brisbane was fit to play after five weeks out. Equally welcoming was the news that the full back Ray Dutton had recovered from the dislocated shoulder sustained in the Monaro game so he would play his first game in New Zealand.

THE LAST HURRAH   The 1970 Tour Down Under

In the newspapers of the 14 July there was yet another reminder that the upcoming Test in Christchurch was not to be broadcast live. It would appear that live rugby league would be broadcast on the coming Saturday but it was to be a club game between Addington and Papanul rather than the Test match on the Sunday. Once again, the home authorities seem to have shot themselves in the foot as they had refused to allow coverage of all three Tests because the fee offered was too low.

Given the record of the Great Britain squad on its arrival into the country you would think the vast majority of sports lovers in New Zealand would have willingly watched the Tests. A great publicity coup was lost frankly through the greed and narrow mindedness of the authorities. Had the game been shown live to a large audience it would have been a great boast for the game. The size of the fee from the television company was a secondary issue really and truthfully.

On the Test front Church and Mountford were looking to make changes for the second encounter. It would appear that the experiment with the young centre Lowther was to be abandoned for the moment as the player was suffering from a bout of the mumps. The press felt that Roger Bailey who had played at stand-off in the first game would move to centre and a new half back pairing was to be selected. Whiteley and Harding on the other hand as they had all the tour said nothing about who was to play or not play. The game in Wellington resulted in the Great Britain side scoring its highest total in a game so far on the tour. They simply out played Wellington winning 60-8. In the process they scored fourteen tries with the two Leeds wingmen having a field day Atkinson crossed for three tries but his mate Smith got five.

What is astonishing was the type of football the tourists produced on a pitch that was a quagmire and got worse as the rain persisted throughout the game. By the end of the game the pitch was literally covered in ankle deep water and resembled a lake rather than a football pitch.

By the time the half time whistle sounded the score line read 41-3 such had been the domination of the visitors. As the players walked off the field Doug Laughton was heard to joke to his team mates "Why don't we declare". What was worrying though was the continuation of the very high penalty count against the Englishmen. Speaking afterward the manager Harding said he was not particularly worried by the penalty count and did not consider it to be a threat in the up coming Test. Coach Whiteley was a little unforgiving of his players telling the reporters:-

"We got a bit slack towards the end. We will need to tighten up before the Test in Christchurch."

This was after the players had scored fourteen tries on a field that resembled a lake by the end of the game. He was a hard task master and was not going to let the players drop their standards while in the Dominion.

The next stop was to be in Christchurch on the South Island east coast. Jack Harding did get some good news prior to the Test when the gate receipts for the first encounter up in Auckland were sent to him £21,335 was the figure of which 65% went into the tour coffers. When that figure was added to the gate receipts for the three Tests in Australia the total rose to £210,000 a very tidy sum and a record for any tour to date.

Once again as the players were preparing for the second Test trouble seemed to be brewing as the New Zealand press reported. They reprinted a report from the Australian Sydney Morning Herald which stated that Phil Lowe, Mal Reilly, Tony Fisher, Alan Hardisty and Roger Millward would be playing their football in Sydney next season. The report went on to say not only that but others would follow as every member of the squad had been approached by Sydney clubs. Negotiations were to continue with the players on their return home.

The reporter stated that both Millward and Reilly had told friends that they would be migrating to Australia next year. The reason for all the speculation was because at the beginning of the tour it was thought that the squad as had been the case on previous tours would be contracted to remain at home for twelve months after the tour ended. However, is seems the only stipulation for this tour was that the players had to return home after the tour ended. There was no mention of just how long they had to remain in England. It was left to the manager Jack Harding to respond to the article and his only comment was that the Sydney clubs would need to pay out hefty transfer fees if they were to get English clubs to release their players. Whiteley would say later to the author:-

"I never felt that was a problem on the tour. I can fully understand why the players were attracting so much interest. Each one of those players had carved out a niche for themselves on the tour. The Australian game was based on power and speed but the English lads promised skill something lacking in the Aussie game at the time. The reporters were always writing about the power of the

Aussies but the skills of the tourists. They brought the English qualities to the fore and the Aussie clubs took notice."

It was a storm in a teacup really, whipped up by a press that wanted something to write about. It was a hindrance when all wanted to concentrate on the upcoming Test but the players were too focused to let it bother them over much.

When Harding and Whiteley announced the second Test side there were a number of changes as there had been in the host side. Keith Hepworth had recovered from the arm injury and would play at scrum half while Ray Dutton replaced Shoebottom at full back. The coach was being true to his words following the first Test defeat in Brisbane that there were no 'ham and eggers' and Test teams would be picked on form. Given that Dutton had kicked nine goals in the Wellington game in atrocious conditions and played very well he was deemed to have earned his place. The players had a bit of light relief before the game when they were taken out of town to do a bit of trap shooting. That is clay pigeon shooting to you and I. It was the first time any leisure activity had seemingly been able to be squeezed into what had been a very tight schedule for the tour. Or at least it was the first that was reported on by the press. There was very little written about what the players did off the field this was probably due to the very tight schedule the players faced.

When the teams went out onto the Orangetheory Stadium in Christchurch on that Sunday the line ups were:-

NEW ZEALAND

Ladner, Orchard, Christian, Bailey, Brereton, Schuster, Carson, Orchard, O'Neil, Gailey, Hibbs, Deacon, Kriletich.

GREAT BRITAIN

Dutton, Smith, Hynes, Myler, Atkinson, Millward, Hepworth, Watson, Fisher, Hartley, Thompson, Laughton, Reilly.

As had been the case in the first encounter it was the Kiwis who started the brighter and with resolute defense and bright attacking play, they kept the record crowd on their toes. The Great Britain defense was tested through out that first forty minutes. After fourteen minutes the full back Ladner dropped a goal to give his side the lead. He repeated the action again fourteen minutes later and the lead was 4-0 to the home side. Five minutes later the crowd was on its feet roaring in excitement as the centre Christian crossed for a try and Ladner added the extra two. The players went off at half time with the remarkable score line of 9-0 in favour of the Kiwis.

Whiteley let rip in the dressing room at what he thought was a poor effort from his players and told them in no uncertain terms what was required of them in the second forty. There were two problems, first was a lack of possession from the scrum due to penalties. Secondly poor handling by the tourists which had given the Kiwis easy yards. Whiteley's comments seemed to work as just five minutes into the second half Myler tore a huge hole in the home defense and laid on a try for Laughton which Dutton converted. Just a few minutes later a Kiwi attack broke down when a pass from one

Orchard brother to the other went astray. The ball was collected by the visitors and passed through half a dozen pairs of hand before the final pass saw the skipper Myler put the ball down over the try line. Once again, the reliable Dutton stepped up and put his side into the lead 10-9. It was a lead they were not to lose.

The English defense had stepped up a gear or two and the only way the Kiwis could make any progress was if the visitors produced a handling error or on the back of Ladner's boot. It seemed that Whiteley's solution to reduce the penalty count was simply to accept that the team would lose the scrums and so ordered Reilly to stand out as an extra stand off. That had two effects firstly it stifled any moves the Kiwis tried in the back line and secondly it gave the side a very aggressive runner if and when Fisher managed to win a scrum. When the tourists had the ball Laughton would often act as an extra three quarter such was the domination of the visiting forwards. At times the tourists would only pack five forwards in the scrum even in defense.

The half backs Millward and Hepworth began to dominate the game with their acceleration and guile and it was no surprise when it was Millward that extended the lead after taking a scoring pass after sixty six minutes. He repeated the dose just six minutes later when Reilly burst through between two defenders and got a pass out to him to go in for another score. With Dutton adding the extras the lead was stretching out. The final try came from a scrum and Hepworth used Reilly to fool the defense to make a break. Once in the clear Hepworth was able to pass the ball to the loose forward who crossed for the final try of the game.

THE LAST HURRAH   *The 1970 Tour Down Under*

The foundation for the victory undoubtable lay in the play of the two props, Watson and Hartley who constantly charged through the defensive line to release Laughton, Thompson and Reilly allowing them to create mayhem in the Kiwi defense. After the game which ended with a score line of 23-9 the Coach told reporters:-

"We suffered a little complacency in the first half but I was confident that New Zealand's nine point lead would not be sufficient to combat the wind in our favour after the break. New Zealand had tremendous courage and undoubted skill but our overall strength told. The Kiwis became very tired knocking our lads down and I knew we would find the gaps."

The only black spot was that once again the penalty count was heavily in favour of the Kiwis 15-6. Whiteley who prided his team's discipline would not have been happy to see them suffer double penalties twice, when players disputed the referee's decision and get marched further down field. The team however had now won four Test matches in a row and that was some feat down under. They did have three more games to complete before they could call it quits and head for home.

The next game was to be out on the west coast of the South Island at Greymouth and it seems the Englishmen fared better with their travel arrangements than did two of the Kiwi boys who were turning out for the Greymouth side. Dixon and Hibbs had played in both the two Tests but Hibbs got the bad news he had been dropped for the third encounter. The players had made their way to the airport to fly to the west coast for the game and it was then it all started going wrong for them.

At the Christchurch airport waiting for the afternoon flight Dixon did not hear the boarding call and was left behind when the airplane took off. Hibbs would have felt his problems were over and Dixon's just beginning. Dixon for his part simply hired a rental car at the airport and began the drive across from the east coast to the west coast. It took him around three hours to cover the 150 mile journey. The aircraft on the other hand with Hibbs on board arrived at the airport at Hokitiki only to find that the weather was so bad the pilot was unable to land and so returned to Christchurch. Hibbs caught a bus and travelled the route Dixon had and arrived hours after Dixon. Such were the vagaries of travel in New Zealand back then.

Mind you the tourists did not fare much better in their travel to the game as the railway line from Christchurch to Greymouth was a single line track that passed through the famous Arthur's Pass. The train passed over the Southern Alps and while quite scenic was just more travel for the players. The journey took around four hours and being single track the service was for that reason somewhat infrequent.

It was expected that the opposition would not be that strong so only three of the players from the second Test were selected for the match Dutton, Atkinson and Hynes were to play but in the team that took to the field that day only the young Phil Lowe and John Ward the Castleford prop had not played in a Test on the tour. The pitch at Wingham Park was covered in mud patches and there was a thunder storm as the game was in progress. You get some idea of just how bad conditions were as at half time the two teams simply changed ends and carried on playing in the pouring rain! It mattered little to the visitors who gave a tremendous exhibition of dry weather rugby league in spite of the greasy ball and treacherous footing. They ran in fifteen tries most of them coming on the back of strong runs from the young Lowe who once in the clear was able to off load at will to the speedier backs. Atkinson kept up his record of scoring a try in all of the games in New Zealand. The end result was 57-2 win for the tourists.

With the third Test due to be played in Auckland the players took to the sky again and once in Auckland prepared for the last big game of the tour. We can see again the selection philosophy that had been adopted all through the tour. Down in the West Coast game at Greymouth Lowe, Ward and Hesketh had put in tremendous performances in atrocious conditions and their reward was a Test cap the only three changes made from the second Test. By doing so Harding and Whiteley ensured every one of the players would return home with a Test cap in their kit bag. John Coffey wrote in The Press of the babe of the party Lowe following the Greymouth game:-

"Lowe's speed and evasiveness in the West Coast match promised to make him one of the prominent players of today."

He certainly was not wrong in his assessment of the Hull lad that afternoon.

Harding and Whiteley were taking nothing for granted with this last Test. The host players would be well aware that a good performance from them in the game could well book them a seat on the flight to England come the end of the season via a spot in the Kiwi World Cup squad that was to be played in the August in England. That being the case it was expected that a more determined Kiwi team would face them that afternoon. The two teams for the final encounter were:-

NEW ZEALAND

Ladner, Lowther, Christian, Redmond, Brereton, Bailey, Carson, Orchard, O'Neil, Gailey, Deacon, Dixon, Kriletich.

GREAT BRITAIN

Dutton, Smith, Hesketh, Myler, Atkinson, Millward, Hepworth, Watson, Fisher, Ward, Lowe, Irving, Reilly.

Once again, the first quarter of the game saw the Kiwis holding their own and a field goal and a penalty from the full back Ladner and a field goal from Millward were the only scores. It was the hosts who were to score the first try when Dutton was caught in possession by Redmond who won the ball and passed out to Bailey and the stand off ran twenty five yards for the score. With Ladner converting the tourists were 9-2 down. Ladner converted another penalty and that was the only other score and took the Kiwis into the half time break 11-2 to the good. It was seemingly a regular occurrence in New Zealand that the tourists would be down in the first half of the Test match.

As in the other Tests once the teams changed ends it was the Great Britain side that took command. They scored their first try after just three minutes of the half when Lowe flew in for a try. Dutton stepped up to close the gap between the sides to 11-7. Next it was the turn of prop Cliff Watson to show why he was considered to be one of the best props if not the best in the game when he used sheer strength to crash over for another converted try and put his side in the lead for the first time. After eighteen minutes Lowe went in for his second score following a lovely break from his second row partner Irving. Just four minutes later it was the wingman Smiths turn and the game as a contest was over.

Hesketh ran through a tiring defense for an unconverted try to make the score 23-11. There was a brief revival from the home side when Orchard crossed and Ladner converted to close the gap to 16-23 with around ten minutes left in the game. Hesketh was forced to leave the field with an injury and Syd Hynes came on as a replacement. From a penalty Millward, Fisher and Reilly combined to send Hepworth diving in for a try. Hynes scored the last try of the game and with Dutton converting both tries the final score was 33-16. The Great Britain side had now won five consecutive Test matches.

There was just one last match to play before the tourists really could let their hair down. If the first Test played on arrival had been a potential banana skin the same could be said of the last game against Auckland. In the past there had been some feisty encounters between these two sides. On the 1954 tour the game had been so brutal it caused the Auckland rugby league authorities to write to the Council in England complaining of the style of play adopted by the Great Britain players. That 1954 tour was marred by complaints of rough not to say dirty play from the visitors. As we know it takes two to tango but it was the tourists who were to carry the bulk of the blame. On returning home there were claims that the Council had drawn up a black list of players who were not to be selected for representative games again. It was a claim the Council always denied.

So, it was against this type of backdrop the Auckland game was played. The authorities had no need to worry as this set of tourists were far and away much better than the hosts that afternoon. They were also far more disciplined in their play than had other touring parties been. It was Millward with three tries that ensured there was to be no slip up in the final game of the tour. In a performance that could not have been scripted better the last try of the tour was to belong to Roger the Dodger. Taking a pass, he flew over the muddy ground at an astonishing speed to score his third try of the game. He left the Auckland players floundering in his wake with not one able to get anywhere near him. The spectators could only stand and marvel had what the little stand off did that afternoon. His scoring in the match took his total points for the tour to one hundred, a remarkable achievement.

Equally pleasing for the coach was that the Auckland side were held try less. They simply did not have the speed or the guile to create a try and the tourists kept their try line intact. Their eight points all came from penalties. Mind you they did have plenty of opportunities as the penalty count at the end stood at 25-7 in favour of the home side. As ever the British defense was rock solid and uncompromising. The players walked off Carlaw Park for the last time on the tour winning 23-8. Pleasing for the manager Jack Harding were the figures produced by the New Zealand authorities for the taking for the seven games.

The gross takings for the tour in New Zealand amounted to £56,000 of which 65% would go into the tour coffers. The figure was £20,000 more than that grossed on the previous Lions tour to the country. There was no doubt the three Test matches had really been money spinners. The team had been in New Zealand just nineteen days and in that time had traveled around 1250 miles in playing the seven games. They had played the game in just the same style that they had on the bone hard Australian pitches and thrilled the crowd by doing so. With the tour now ended on the playing front it was time for the squad to pack up and fly to Sydney, there they would catch a flight back home to England.

CHAPTER FIVE

The Tour aftermath

When the players arrived back in Sydney both Jack Harding and Johnny Whiteley were as was to be expected in demand from members of the press, It was a surprise to no one given the success of the tour but also because of the speculation regarding which players would be returning soon to play for clubs in Sydney. The Rugby League News of the 1 August carried an interview with Johnny Whiteley. What he had to say proved to be very farsighted and scary in its accuracy with regard to the Australians, frighteningly so:-

"You have much talent. There is talent, talent everywhere. We saw it at the start of the tour in Darwin and we have seen it everywhere.

You have to do some thinking about method; there are great players yet to be replaced. But you will find them- there is so much latent talent about."

There is little doubt that Whiteley was speaking with the voice of authority as his standing in Australia was at an all time high. After all he had masterminded an Ashes winning squad that had played the game at the highest level. Brilliant football with the ball in hand, tough uncompromising defense when the opposition were in possession of the ball. He had adapted his players not only to the local conditions but also to the relatively new four tackle rule that the game was playing under. He had also adapted his players to deal with 'opposition of the rugged type.' He went on to say of the Australian authorities:-

"I have no doubt your people will have the game back on the right track before long. It is not only that you have such great numbers to work on, what with schoolboys, juniors and young players in your clubs, but also there is so much promising talent about the place.

Teams will need speed-perhaps more so and with your good weather and firm grounds you can exploit speed."

When you look at what he said it is almost as if he had a crystal ball and was able to look into the future. The Australians went on to win the World Cup that same year against all the odds. They also went on to dominate the international game from that point on with power and pace we could not match.

There is little doubt that the success of the tour was a great boast for the game in England but the four tackle rule was provoking a great deal of discussion. There were some looking to bring in a little more elasticity into the new rule without stifling the creativity in the game particularly in Australia. The noted English journalist Joe Humphreys hit the nail on the head when he wrote:-

"We cannot understand talk of panic kicking on the fourth tackle. If your team wants to kick, they can do so on the first, second or third tackle and not keep it every time to the fourth with the opposition prepared."

With his experienced eye Humphreys was able to observe why the Englishmen had exploited the new rule better than the Australians. They were relying on backing up the player with the ball who was prepared to off load the ball knowing some one would be in support. The Aussies on the other hand relied on players crashing through with the ball with little or no thought to off loading the ball. They were very insightful words back then. Look at the game today particularly in Australia once we moved to a six tackle game. We get five drives from players crashing through with no intention of passing the ball and then a kick. There is no doubt that the new rule was very demanding on players fitness and coaching tactics. Whiteley exploited the new rule to perfection simply because he demanded greater fitness from his players than had generally been the rule in the unlimited tackle era back in England.

Later the great Australian coach Jack Gibson would travel over to the United States to study the American Football game with its four downs. Gibson like Whiteley saw the demands the new rules made on players, he also saw that it was power and strength that worked in the American game and it was that which would work in the Australian game. Many of the innovations he introduced into the Australian game are still with us today.

In that same issue of the Rugby League News the manager Jack Harding gave his thoughts on the tour stating that he was delighted that every player in the squad had won a Test cap. Whiteley was quick to point out that it was not a case of taking any opposition lightly rather that the resources and the 'form' was present in the squad. Harding was even more delighted with the tour profits generated telling reporters:-

"The tour profits will be around £130,000 and to this will be added the television rights from the Australian Test which should take the figure out to a profit of around £150,000."

That would have been music to the ears of the players as it transferred into a tour bonus of nearly £1,000 per player. Not a bad return for ten or more weeks work you may well think. Wingman Alan Smith revealed to the author the final figure was a little less:-

"The statement I received from Bill Fallowfield at the Rugby League showed the share of the profits to the players came to £25,587. That came to £984-2s-2d each. The final pay cheque for the tour was less any private drawings taken by players on tour. Most of us were left with very little, but worth every penny. I drew some £700 while I was on tour so got a cheque for just £284-2s-2d."

When you look at the figures two things become apparent. First, that the final cheque is not that great but then all accommodation and travel was paid for so the players did not have to fork out for that. Secondly, on other previous tours in earlier times a daily allowance was paid to players when in the countries and a full tour bonus was paid to players at the end of the trip. Having said all that Smith perhaps summed up best the feelings of the players "worth every penny."

While in Sydney and before heading for the airport and a flight home the coach Whiteley and skipper Frank Myler along with a number of the players went down to Moore Park. There they attended a Sydney Convent Schools event and spent time with the youngsters. The coach presented officials with two rugby balls signed by all the tour squad. The balls were raffled off later to raise funds for the schoolboy referee's society. It was a nice touch and one that pleased the authorities in Sydney.

The coach did get one thing very wrong but through no fault of his when he told reporters:-

"With so many of our players on the young side, this team should provide the basis of our next touring side here four years hence."

Little did he or anyone else for that matter realise that players of the caliber of Reilly, Lowe, and Watson would be lost to the Australian game. Others would follow and with the six tackle rule we still persisted with trying to use guile rather than power and pace. We had an influx of Australian coaches into our game that reinforced the belief that what was needed was to run at the man rather than at the gaps in the defensive line. Games were to be won by pace and power and the team that was the fittest at the end of eighty minutes. The Aussies as Whiteley had predicted developed players of greater pace and power than the English game did and we all know the result of that approach.

Back home the clubs were worried more about what they considered to be illegal approaches to their players. It had long been seen as a problem by clubs that their players would be attracted to the lifestyle and climate they were to experience down in Sydney. It was for that reason that on previous tours there had been an agreement between England and Australia that players from either country selected to go on tour could not be signed by a club until a period of two years had elapsed following the tour. It would seem no such contract proviso had been included in the present tour. All that was required of players was that they return home to England when the tour ended. It was a mistake that had many clubs up in arms at the time.

So worried were English clubs about the illegal approaches to their players as they saw it that they had requested a meeting in the coming August to discuss the matter. They were of the opinion that a good number of their players had been approached by Sydney clubs and were thinking of returning to Sydney if terms could be arranged. That was probably the case truth be known. North Sydney, South Sydney, St. George, Penrith and Cronulla were clubs that it was believed had approached the tourists. This was a problem as was said that was not new it had caused problems way back in 1912 and had led to the very acrimonious 1914 tour which saw the 'Rorke's Drift Test.

Frawley had signed a three year contract with Warrington only to return home after one year. His club Eastern Suburbs had allowed him to play for them knowing he was a Warrington player. Frawley had been selected to tour England on the 1911-12 tour the dispute involving Warrington and Eastern Suburbs caused Warrington to refuse permission for the player to play during the early part of the tour. While on tour Dan Frawley signed a new contract with Warrington only to renege on the club once more and return home at the tours end and continue playing for Eastern Suburbs. The ill feeling this generated carried forward to the 1914 tour down under which almost did not take place and the stand off between the two countries prior to the now famous third Test won by the visitors. The English clubs had if nothing else long memories.

Following that report on the 29 July in the Canberra Times detailing the approaches, the newspaper followed it up the following day with a further report which stated that a meeting had been arranged in Leeds for the 20 August. The

Leeds club were particularly incensed as they believed four of their players had been illegally approached. The ever calm head of Council Secretary Bill Fallowfield seemed to come up with one obvious solution:-

"The most simple solution would be for the Council to say it would grant clearances only in exceptional circumstances and only if the players club raised no objections."

Some clubs stated they would not grant any player a transfer but such action would only be effective if it was accepted by the Aussie clubs which seems to be in some doubt. If Australian clubs took the view that the player was in Australia and playing for them, should the English club want to go to court to challenge them, so be it.

There is no doubt that there was some confusion in this area particularly with the English clubs. There is little doubt that a good many of the tourists were approached by Australian clubs and made offers. The question is were those offers for players to move permanently to Australia or to play for clubs during the English close season? The Canberra Times on the 31 July carried an article concerning the then Castleford skipper Alan Hardisty who had received an offer from the Penrith club. When talking to the reporters at Sydney Airport Hardisty told them:-

"I will have to see what my club says before taking any action, but I would like to go to Australia for a season next February. Unfortunately, if I leave then it will mean leaving Castleford in the middle of their cup commitments."

The Castleford vice-chairman Bill Broxon responded in much the same manner as the Leeds Club officials had, saying there was no way they would allow any player to leave the club. Hardisty told reporters he intended to speak to the club directors when he returned home saying:-

"I have given long service to the club, and now there is the chance of a big reward from football. I think the club should let me go."

Sadly the club did not as Hardisty revealed to the author and he also revealed that he had received an offer back in 1966 while on his first tour down under:-

"In 1966 the St George club wanted me to go down and play the English close season with them. I would have loved to play for them at the time they had the likes of Gasnier and Langlands in the side and won I think ten Grand Finals. Penrith approached me in 1970 to play again in the close season but the club said no. I did go to Australia but it was when I had retired. I played a season as player/coach at the Brothers club up in Rockhampton in Queensland."

That same article also named other players believed to have been made offers by Australian clubs including Reilly, Hynes and Shoebottom. It must be stressed that what is not known is whether these were offers to play during the close season or on a permanent basis. There is one thing that was certain and that was the clubs in England were really running scared, feeling that a number of top players could well simply immigrate down under and by doing so would be holding clubs to ransom. It is a moot point as to if the Aussie clubs would have played them in spite of the players being under contract to their clubs in England but the feeling at the time was that they would do so. After all they had history in that area.

There is no doubt that these problems took more than a little of the shine off the return home of the player on that Thursday the 30 July as the Secretary Bill Fallowfield noted:-

"It had been a good tour but the edge has been spoiled by the alleged offers made to some of our players by Australian clubs. No doubt the Rugby League Council will have something to say about these offers when they meet."

It is not known just what Council decided but what we did see in later seasons was a plethora of players going down under for short contracts during our close season and the Aussies doing the same. It certainly got the backs up of the clubs and Council as we shall see.

The meeting was set for Thursday the 20 August and at that meeting the manager of the tour Jack Harding was due to give his tour report. Certainly, there were three things that Council would be looking at very carefully. One was the controversy that had surrounded Reilly both in Queensland and down in Sydney. Secondly the alleged illegal approaches made to players by Australian clubs. Finally, the financial problems associated with the television rights to the three Test matches in Australia. Reilly certainly would have forfeited some of his tour bonus that is for sure following his indiscretions. However, with the Ashes back in English hands there is no doubt Reilly would have been forgiven any indiscretions.

With regard to the illegal approaches the Council was less than happy with such matters and had been for a good deal of time. It would be true to say relationships between the two countries authorities were somewhat strained and the recent actions had done nothing to ease the situation. The problem was the attitude of the Australian clubs who generally speaking signed players to year or season long contracts. They also had in place residential rules which stated that a player could only play for the club in the district he was living in, while in Sydney. In England when a player signed for his club, he signed a contract for life or until the club struck him off their register. That was why they were able to demand a transfer fee for a player something a little alien to the Aussies.

Those two issues while in themselves serious paled into insignificance against the main topic on the agenda, namely the television rights for the Test matches or more accurately the financial arrangements between the Australian game and the television companies. The Council was "aggrieved" that they had not been consulted about the television coverage of tour matches. Bill Fallowfield reported:-

"We did not know that games were to be televised or that the fees had been agreed on. There should have been a joint agreement between the two bodies. We have taken it up with the Australian League in correspondence."

Fallowfield did have a point as it turned out the game played up in Newcastle by the tourists was televised and the Aussies did not even know it was being televised and the League got no broadcasting fee for the match. With Jack Harding in the country good manners dictated that he should at least have been involved in the financial negotiations regarding the televising of the three Test matches. Sadly, that proved not to be the case and it was this that had angered Council. The unfortunate thing was that all of this bickering was reported by the press and what got lost in the process is just what the twenty six players had achieved on that tour.

Instead of lauding the efforts of the players in bringing back The Ashes the bigger story was the washing of the game's dirty linen in public sadly not for the only time in the game. Little did anyone know at the time but it would be the last occasion the home side would lift the Ashes trophy either at home or on future tours. For that reason the players on that tour never really received the accoladed they deserved. They were not fated then and have never really been fated since by the game. With the advent of Super League the feeling is that what transpired in this great game before Super League is no longer of any importance. It was Henry Ford who famously said that "History is Bunk" unfortunately it is a phrase that todays officials in the game seem to be subscribing!

CHAPTER SIX

The Tour assessed

There is no doubt that the 1970 tour was the most successful tour ever down to Australia and New Zealand on so many levels. It was a relatively short tour being just a day over ten weeks long from leaving Manchester to its return. It resulted in record profits coming in at around £150,000 and with it record bonuses for the players. Its success was however much more than that. It provided a fillip that our domestic game needed at the time when it was struggling on and off the field and it brought a wealth of young talent into the game. Inevitably it also saw players, great players at that, leave the international scene. It also had the effect of seeing the demise of the unlimited tackles era the game had experience for so long that had led to claims that the game was becoming dull and boring!

One of the problems experienced with modern travel was that players were hard pressed to get good quality training sessions in due to the short turn round times between games at the various venues. Equally important was that there was little leisure time built into the tour schedule. Unlike in the past when tours were much longer and the players were able to see and enjoy much more of the two countries and the hospitality offered to them by the people.

When a tour such as this is assessed, given just how successful it turned out to be it is difficult to highlight this player or that player who had contributed so much to the success of the visit. The coach Johnny Whiteley had no such trouble when talking to the author and was asked which player or players stood out for him during the tour.

"There is no doubt in my mind who was my player of that tour and that was Cliff Watson. He was the corner stone of our players. He had come from London up to Saints. When he went down to Australia, he was probably the best prop in the world. I will tell you this, on tour he became a colossus. He rose in stature as a player and the respect that the players had for him grew week on week.

Dennis Hartley joined Cliff in that respect and proved to be another tough English prop on that trip. The pair of them never once took a backward step in any game. They were the cornerstones of our pack. With Tony Fisher in the middle you really did not need the other three forwards, they could simply go and play the skillful football knowing those three in the front row would handle whatever came at them.

I also felt that Frank Myler was a wonderful captain of the side not just on the field but off the field as well. People forget that we had not a lot of time for the players to get to know each other and each others game. Frank was marvelous and fully deserved to pick up the Ashes for us. We had little Roger Millward who was great he was darting here and there during games and the opposition could not handle him."

It must be said that Whiteley was not alone in his views regarding Watson's contribution on the tour. In an article in The Rugby League News on the day of the third Test the reporter had this to say:-

"It is doubtful if any visiting player has had a greater influence on the tour overall than the experienced and embattled prop Cliff Watson. He is a rugged player and was involved in a bad incident in the Brisbane Test. But he has been a staunch and uncompromising player for Britain and knowledgeable with it."

In the same article the writer was of the opinion that win or lose the tour would be deemed a success simply because of the way the tourists had played the game. Also, for the players it had unearthed:-

"'Ashes' or not this 1970 combination will take back to England a number of young players advanced by experience. Amongst them are forwards Malcolm Reilly, Jim Thompson (tenacious tackler), Bob Irving and the 16 stone Phil Lowe who missed the Tests but is one for the future.

Five-eighth Roger Millward after his inspired performance in the second Test and fast clever wingman John Atkinson will be remembered as 'clear cut' successes.

Also, half back Barry Seabourne whose reputation as a young footballer of 'character' preceded him from Leeds but a leg injury persisted."

This was praise indeed from an Australian rugby league writer.

It is difficult to pick out any one player as so many of them performed so well. Terry Price bought into the ethos of the squad and got himself fitter than he had ever been and put in some superb performances as the tour went on. Ray Dutton suffered from a dislocated shoulder yet came back and won a Test cap in New Zealand. The light weight Derek Edwards performed well but as Whiteley revealed he was a player who suffered greatly from home sickness. He was never really fully at ease on tour much preferring to be back home and yet he also performed well at the very highest level.

The tour brought Roger Millward to the fore on the world stage along with Syd Hynes, Smith and Atkinson. Chris Hesketh would captain the tourists on the 1974 tour down under. Mick Shoebottom was a real find and helped win the second Test in Sydney. Sadly, injury robbed the game of him at the height of his career really as has been mentioned earlier. Frank Myler had experienced a stellar career in the game at both club and international level. It was a fitting end to his international career that he would lift the Ashes in Australia. Clive Sullivan was a wingman of great quality but it must be said that Smith and Atkinson were nothing short of outstanding in every game they played so it is little wonder Sullivan had to take second place.

Alan Hardisty a star in his own right who had achieved all the game had to offer he was to be replaced by a player of world class in Millward. He had gone on the tour in truth as the first choice stand off in the minds of many in the game. Perhaps under a lesser coach than Whiteley and his no 'ham and eggers' approach, he would have remained so. On this tour it was form that mattered more than reputation. If you are to be replaced is there any better way to bow out of the international scene than to be replaced by Roger the Dodger?

On the tour the nuggety Castleford scrum half Keith Hepworth proved that he could perform as well at international level as he had been doing for years for the Castleford club. He showed quite clearly that he was not only the top scrum half in the English game at the time but also on the world stage. Barry Seabourne suffered from injury on the trip and the form shown by Hepworth but the England captain was also to gain a cap against the Kiwis. Who knows just what he would have achieved but for the leg injury that took so long to heal while he was in Australia.

When if ever did the game have two loose forwards of the quality of Doug Laughton and Mal Reilly playing at the same time. They were players of immense talent capable of winning a game on their own when they had the ball in hand and saving a game when it came to defending. Certainly, Reilly lived up to the hype and really did match Vince Karalius although not the Wild Bull he was certainly wild. He was though a player who knew the game inside out and did so while so young. Laughton was the thinking mans loose forward who could play the game whichever way the opposition wanted.

When you look at the second row forwards in that squad Robinson was just twenty five and yet was making his second trip down under. The other three, well Bob Irving was the old man of the three at just twenty two while the tackling machine that was the Featherstone Rovers player Jimmy Thompson was only twenty one. He came of age on the tour especially in the second and third Test matches against the Aussies. The baby of the whole squad was the Hull KR lad Phil Lowe at just twenty and yet he also was not out of place at the very top level of the game. All would go on to have great careers in the game.

When you consider the prop forwards Cliff Watson was already considered to be one of the best if not the best prop in the world. All thought Dennis Hartley was supposed to be over the hill at thirty four years of age the problem was that someone forgot to tell Dennis and so he trampled all over the opposition on the tour. John Ward sadly was somewhat overshadowed by Watson and Hartley but performed well and added a Great Britain cap to his England caps. The young inexperienced Leigh prop Dave Chisnall also collected a Great Britain cap, grew immensely as a player on the tour and on returning home asked Leigh for a transfer and went on to have a great career with Warrington amongst a number of clubs. He would go on to play for and gained five England caps.

The two hookers were from opposite ends of the spectrum in truth. Flanagan had earned the nickname 'Flash' from his playing style. He had begun the tour as first choice hooker in the mind of many. He did seem to get on the wrong side of the referees with monotonous regularity whenever he played with his hooking style. Tony Fisher was noted more for his no nonsense approach to the game based on the most rugged of defense and an ability to take the ball up. With him in the side Watson and Hartley became more potent as an attacking and defensive force. As the tour progressed, he became the first choice hooker for Whiteley.

The Test front row of Watson, Fisher and Hartley was the perfect example of the view that 'the whole was greater than the sum of its parts'. Or as Whiteley put it, far more simply the three of them together were the last time this country had a world class front row. Whiteley regarded Watson and the Wigan player Brian McTigue as the best two props he had ever seen and once told the author that with Fisher in the middle you would not need the back three to win any game.

When you look at the tour in terms of statistics the players were away from home seventy one days just over ten weeks. In that time, they played twenty four games winning twenty two, drawing one and losing one. That equates to an average of one game every three days or so. God alone knows what the present day players would do faced with such a schedule. During the time they were in Australia and New Zealand they travelled around 8750 miles. It was a phenomenal effort of organization, stamina, patience and stoicism from all concerned and at the end of it all they brought home a small gold trophy, the Ashes Cup. They brought home a great deal more than that however, they returned pride to the rugby league heartland in the north of England.

The sad thing is that the game did not build on what had been achieved. Players of the likes of Watson, Reilly, and Lowe were allowed to move down under. The coach was allowed to drift away from the international scene thus the game lost a great deal of expertise at the international level. Once the Australians got to grips with the now six tackle game, they began to dominate the game internationally. In order to compete with them the feeling was that we needed to bring in not only Australian coaches but Australian players who could implement the game plan these coaches wanted to play.

The result was a slow and steady decline in the skill factors of the English game and the English players the one thing we were much better at than the Australians. When you look at the game today both here and down under it is purely and simply an Australian model. We see five drives and a kick, teams playing simply for field position. Players coached to run at the man rather than the gap and never off load as it could result in an error the thing coaches these days hate more than anything else. It is a game of pace and power and just as Whiteley had predicted back in 1970 the Australian game was more suited to that style of play than were the English. He also was spot on with the opinion that the new rules were more demanding on the fitness of players than had been the old unlimited tackles rule.

The 1970 touring team played fast, open attractive rugby league and did so under a four tackle rule. Their game was based on the notion of players backing up the ball carrier at all times. The ball carrier for his part knew that there would always be players supporting him so he was constantly looking to off load the ball. The big question is simply will we ever see the likes of that style of play again in our game?

(The players return to Manchester with the Ashes Trophy John Whiteley and Jack Harding hold it aloft)

THE LAST HURRAH *The 1970 Tour Down Under*

Little did any one realise that the above photograph at Manchester Airport on that July morning would record the last time the English game was to experience success against the Australians in a three match Test series. The trophy they are proudly holding aloft now resided in the NRL Museum down in Sydney. It seems that it is destined to remain there as we no longer have 'Ashes' tours so there is no opportunity for the Great Britain team ever to regain it.

PERSONAL TOUR RECOLLECTIONS
Tony Fisher - Bradford Northern

When I got selected to go on that tour I really was over the moon it was something I had never even thought of when I started in the game. When I came into the game, I was actually serving in the RAF Regiment. I had been out in South Africa and then I was transferred to Malaysia to the Butterworth Airfield. We were attached to the Royal Australian Air Force and were charged with providing protection for the airfield. I had played rugby union back in Wales but played a lot more out in Malaysia and there were a lot of Aussies playing there. They were good hard players and I learned a great deal from playing with and against them.

I was home on leave and my Brother Edwal was playing for Bradford Northern at the time. He asked me to go to training with him so I went along to training one night. The club offered me three trials which I agreed to play. The problem was that after the second one they said I had played the best trial games they had ever seen. They wanted to sign me there and then. I told them that I was in the RAF Regiment so could not sign for the club. The club directors simply said, 'Do not worry we will just buy you out,' which they did.

When I got to Australia it was exceptional as I was able to meet up with lots of the Aussies I had served with in Malaysia. I was invited to BBQ's here there and everywhere. I went down to Kangaroo Valley South of Sydney to meet up with a great mate from the services. People had told me before I left England that I was going to be a country boy, one of those players who only played in the mid week country games. It seemed that had been the normal way of things on other tours. It did not bother me I was just going to play as well as I could.

I did not get into the Test side for the first Test up in Brisbane when we got beaten badly and so I thought I may be in with a chance in the Second Test. Sure enough I got picked and I had Dennis Hartley on one side and Cliff Watson on the other. I can tell you this when I was between those two in the scrum, I could do anything I wanted. You have to remember in those days the front row was more than a bit of a contest Cliff and Dennis were the best, knew it, and proved it in the two Tests I played with them in Australia. There was a lot of stuff going on in the scrums back then but I knew those two would look after me which they did.

When we won the third game and with it the Ashes it was the most wonderful day. There was no way we were going to lose the game that afternoon. Cliff and Dennis were outstanding both in the scrum and in the loose. We had Jimmy Thompson who tackled anything that moved that day and Mal Reilly was absolutely marvelous. We were so good that afternoon we did not really need Doug Laughton who was the football brains in the pack he spent most of the game out in the three quarter line. The thing was that Johnny Whiteley knew what to do, what was needed and made sure we knew what we had to do.

When we went down to New Zealand, we never really trained that much we did a lot of ball work because Johnny knew we did not need it. We were very fit And Johnny knew it. He knew every player and what he wanted from them. We won the three Tests down in New Zealand in fact we won all our games. The only game we lost was that first Test. Following that tour my playing career never looked back. My coaching career was a different story.

We did not build on that tour because we lost players to Australia but those players who remained were never given an opportunity to coach at the top level when they finished playing. I coached lower level clubs but never got the chance at big clubs like Leeds. I think there was a bit of the not what you know but who you know in the game when it came to selecting a coach for the big clubs. I also found that more and more as time went on players were dictating rather than the coach. You had to watch what you said to players not like when I was playing.

When I signed for Leeds Rocky Turner was the coach and I remember after one game I played I had lost the scrums. In the dressing room after the game Rocky told me 'I brought you here to win the ball for us that is your job if you do not do it again you will be out'. Now you have to be so polite or players will walk away. We lost a good deal of experience in our game from players on that tour who never got the opportunity at the highest level to coach the game. They were players who had done it at the highest level on the field but never were given an opportunity to show if they could do it as a coach.

Alan Hardisty - Castleford

I had been selected to go on the 1966 tour and had a great time in Australia and New Zealand. When I found out that I had been selected to go on tour again in 1970 I was over the moon I can tell you. I really feel for the players of today as they never get the opportunity to go on the long tours we went on so are missing a great deal. It really was the pinnacle of a players' career in my day. The tours came round every four years and I was lucky enough to go on two of them.

The coach Johnny Whiteley was excellent and he made it clear there was to be only one squad, when I went in 1966 the first and second teams were practically decided before we even set foot in Australia. I mean I was selected as first choice stand off on the 1970 tour but Roger Millward replaced me in the second Test, he really was a world class player. If you were on top of your game you were picked with Whiteley.

I am not one for remembering individual games I was involved in but we did play well on that tour. After the first Test when the team meeting was held it was really the forwards that took the decision not to take a backward step. We backs had nothing to do with that, it was the job of the pack to take us forward all we as backs did was simple score the tries when the opportunities came along. We could only do that if the forwards got the ball for us. The forwards decided following that meeting that they would play the game which ever way the opposition wanted it. For us backs it made little difference to what we had to do, we just had to score the points. We had one job and that was to make the best use of the opportunities that the forwards made for us.

It is true Mal Reilly got into a spot of bother but boy what a player he was on that tour and later. I had the luxury of playing along side him at Castleford. He was a dedicated all action man so it is not surprising trouble seemed to find him. I would rather have played with him than play against him I can tell you.

A lot is talked about having to adjust to the differing conditions down there but players should be good enough to adjust to those conditions. In Australia it was the bone hard pitches that were the problem as we never got those sort of grounds here. You got blisters on the feet and burns on your knees when you got tackled. The hard grounds were a problem but the players quickly got used to them That was the most successful tour ever and you have to ask why we never won the Ashes again after 1970.

The Aussies always played a power and pace game against you. When I went down in 1966 Tommy Bishop and I quickly saw that and we started to put little grubber kicks in behind then to make them turn around or make them think twice about coming up so quickly. The Aussies had a big advantage in the power and pace game but we had ball playing forwards and the backs had far more football skills with runaround plays and kicks. Where we went wrong was in playing the Australian style of game. It is so predictable and boring five drives and a kick these days. We will never beat the Aussies playing their type of game we have to match them in the power game but we should still be looking to use the ball playing skills we once had. We seem to spend all our time now coaching those skills out of our players.

Keith Hepworth - Castleford

It was the best tour ever you know as we only lost one game, drew one and won the rest. When we were up in Queensland, we were beating everyone, we were a cut above the rest of the other teams at that time. I think when the first Test came around our coach Johnny Whiteley was conned into thinking we were good enough to win by the Aussie press. They were making us favourites to win that first Test but we were not ready. Johnny said that he had been conned a bit but it was not going to happen again. He said that he was going to stick by what he knew. We never looked like getting beaten after that first Test.

On that tour Cliff Watson, Tony Fisher, Dennis Hartley and Mal Reilly were from another planet believe me. That Test team had it all, with Johnny as the coach, Jim Thompson the Featherstone lad he would tackle all day and all night if that was what was needed. Laughton was a footballer but was not going to shirk if the going got tough. The full back Terry Price was an excellent goal kicker but did not have the pace needed at Test level. If anyone got through the defensive line they could leave him for dead with pace. When we won the Ashes on that Saturday It was an excellent day all round. I think the Aussies appreciated what we had done and the way we did it.

We were a good side and everybody had a good relationship, the Lancashire lads and the Yorkshire lads got on well. From my point of view playing behind that Test pack allowed me to play my game. Watson, Hartley and Fisher crickey they were three bloody hard cases I can tell you. Mal well he was on another level in Australia. I had seen the lad come to

Castleford as a teenager who even then thought he was the best. He was sixteen or seventeen and I remember we went over to play St. Helens and my mate Alex Murphy met up with Mal for the first time. He said to me during the game who the hell is that lad where did he come from. When I told him Mal was just a teenager he said bloody hell he has no fear of anyone has he, Murphy could not believe how old he was. He was right because Mal slaughtered some of the big names he played against here and on that tour.

What people forget is that the backs were not too bad either we had Syd Hynes and Frank Myler in the centres and the two Leeds lads Atkinson and Smith on the wings with Roger at stand off. That team really did have it all I would say. Frank was a great captain he had a quiet way about him but led us well.

Widnes were the team to beat back then and if you went there and won you knew you had been in a hard game. If you lost you knew you had been given a good hiding. It did not matter who you played to Mal they were all the same he went out and played like only Mal could. We won the second and third Tests as you know and then we went over to New Zealand. We won the first Test and then travelled around the country playing.

You know all of the players on that tour did not ever want to lose they only ever wanted to win. I remember we played one game there in a down pour and the ground was a mud bath. I think the referee blew up early that afternoon simply because you could not tell who was who as we were all covered in mud. We won the other two Tests in New Zealand so had a clean sweep. As I said we never looked like ever getting beat and were always a cut above every team we played.

When I got home, things were changing at Castleford Alan Hardisty went to Leeds and then I followed him. When you change clubs it can give you a new lease of life. I do remember that soon after I had gone to Leeds we played Castleford and during the game Dennis Hartley knocked two or three of my teeth out. I saw him coming and we clashed heads. In the players lounge after the game I said to him bloody hell mate what was going on out there. He came over to me and put his arm round me and said sorry old lad. Then he whispered in my ear but I hate Leeds. There was me spitting blood at the time and all he could say was he did not like Leeds.

When we got home from that tour it was the World Cup and we were favourites to win after winning down in Australia. Sadly, we got beaten in the final by the Aussies. I think in one game if New Zealand had won the game with a few more points we would have played them in the final and that would have been an easier game. As it was Australia made it to the final on points difference. When that competition ended that was the end of my international career. I went on to play for Hull then I finished.

I do like this Summer rugby I think it is great. When I was playing you played in all sorts of weather and on all sorts of pitches. Wind, rain, hail, snow or frost it made no difference you had to play. Now players go out in good weather and on good pitches which allows them to play the game better. I would have loved to play summer rugby.

Syd Hynes – Leeds

I hoped that I would get picked for the tour but really you never knew for certain until you got the call from the Rugby League officials. I was delighted when I got told I was going down to Australia. We flew down and landed in Darwin at 4.00am in the morning and the temperature was 41 degrees it was a bit of a shock to the system.

I was not picked for the first Test Mick Shoebottom got the nod. Luckily for me but not for the squad we got beaten in that Test. As a result, when the second Test came around in Sydney, I was picked to play in the centre. We played well that day and in the second half I kicked a drop goal to stretch our lead. A couple of minutes later I was taking the ball up and Artie Beetson caught me late on the side of the jaw with his elbow. He knocked out my wisdom teeth which did not please me. Back in those days if you could not look after yourself in the game you were dead. I remember I aimed a kick at Beetson while I was on the floor but I missed him.

Next thing I see is the touch judge running on waving his flag. He told the referee that I had kicked Beetson, I said I missed him sir but the referee sent me off. When you were on tour and had to go to the judiciary, they would never suspend you so that you missed a Test match. They would be happy to make you miss a mid-week game but not a big game. That was my experience anyway. When we won the Ashes I would say that was the best experience of my career. We simply out played them that afternoon and they and the crowd knew it. It was the referee that kept the Aussies in the game that afternoon. He kept giving them penalties and the full back kept kicking the two points.

When we were in New Zealand we had played in Christchurch and had then to travel over to Greymouth. We travelled by train and it was a single line it took us a while to get there. When we went out to play it looked like we had walked onto a farmer's field rather that a football field. I do remember on the way back the train driver had a crate of beer with him in the cab which he drank on the way back to Christchurch. It was the funniest thing I have ever seen.

There were a lot of the players on that tour who were approached by Australian clubs to go and play for them. Some clubs wanted them for an English closed season some permanently. In my case the Eastern Suburbs club wanted to sign me. At the time I was probably the best centre in the world on form and that is what attracted Easts. They actually came over to England to try to sign me and offered me £3,000 a season. That was a lot more than Leeds were paying me I can tell you. The club would not let me go or they would release me providing Easts paid a £25,000 transfer fee for me. There was no way they were ever going to do that. It was a shame really as I really wanted to play in Sydney.

When I look at the game today that I see on television in England and the game here in Australia there is no comparison. The rugby league I see in Sydney is hard and fast. It is all power and strength from the first minute to the last. When I look at the English game it looks like a game of touch and pass to me. We will never beat the Aussies again in my opinion while we play that sort of game. You need to match the Aussies in the forwards before you can start to beat them with football and the players in England do not seem to be able to match the Aussies up front. We need power and speed and players that can keep it up the whole game if we are ever to beat the Aussies again.

*(**Hynes now lives in Perth in Western Australia**)*

Malcolm Reilly - Castleford

I got into all kinds of trouble and was lucky I didn't get sent home from the tour. The captain, Frank Myler, Cliff Watson and the coach, Johnny Whiteley went in to bat for me and I will be forever grateful for their loyalty. I won't go into details it did go to the high court and I was acquitted. One funny incident was on the tarmac at Brisbane airport where a very attractive lady tried to serve a writ on me. Cliff Watson realised what was happening and quickly moved me onto the plane. She asked the crew to announce over the tannoy 'could Mr Reilly please press his call button'. All 25 members of the squad pressed their call button. The lady left in despair. I was both frightened and elated. If she had served the writ, I wouldn't have been allowed to leave Brisbane. On returning a number of players, myself included, left the U.K and went down under to join Aussie clubs. Bill Ashurst and Cliff Watson joined Cronulla and Penrith and Phil Lowe went to Manly. Rugby League is the major sport in N.S.W. We had a great international squad in 1970. I had 7 years as international coach and we did have some success but I do think R.L in this country is not on the same scale as in Sydney, Brisbane and Australia in general. Hence in recent times some of our players have chosen to play in the Aussie comp. I think that playing down under in their domestic comp does enhance the prospects of the national side but at the same time depleting R.L in this country.

Jimmy Thompson - Featherstone Rovers

Memories of 1970 Ashes Tour to Australia and New Zealand

As 21 year old and the only player from Featherstone, I went on this tour not knowing many players. I wasn't selected in the first batch of players and was known as a 'ham and egger', which was the term used for players who would probably not be in the first team squad but played in minor matches. As it worked out, I missed only one match the whole tour and that was the only match we lost that one being the first Test.

I remember landing in Darwin and a few hours later playing a match, no consideration was taken for the time difference, the humid weather conditions or the long flight, it was a case of we're here get playing.

Every day followed a schedule of training or playing matches and functions in the evening. I shared a room with Phil Lowe who played for Hull KR and spent most of the tour with him.

I am not one of the players who can recollect any particular match or event, they all run into one to be honest, but I do have recollections of the third Test and the build up to it, when we won the Ashes.

I never gave it a great deal of thought at the time, but have since thought about the fact that that team were never given any recognition in the form of a medal or otherwise for this tremendous achievement. It hasn't been done since and is 50 years next year since it happened.

Alan Smith - Leeds

When the 1970 touring party met at Manchester Airport in May to fly down to Heathrow, it was, not only the gathering of 26 of the best players to take on Australia and New Zealand, but individuals who had during the past season raged war against one another in some of the most spectacular and fiercest games the modern game has seen since the introduction of the four or six tackle rule. When we were thrust together on the aircraft you could feel the tension and the mood of earlier battles. Responsible for the unity of us all, just two of the greatest respected individuals in Johnny Whiteley coach and Jack Harding manager. We landed in Darwin at 5.30 am on the 22nd May. At 8.30pm that same day we played our first game against The Northern Territory, Darwin, winning the game comfortably despite a long tiring journey and in them days we were not sure what jet lag was.

The next day we flew down to Townsville where they had declared a local holiday on the 24th to welcome and watch all their local talent take on the Poms. In the first half we built up a confident 23 points to nil lead. In the second half we all discovered jet lag. They ran us ragged building up 20 points and things were not looking or feeling good. Until at this point I witnessed the first coming together of a team. Our pack took control of the "local talent" and crushed any further threat amiably assisted by us backs and they did not score another point.

Down to Rockhampton (win) and then to Brisbane building up an early reputation for the brand of rugby these Poms were playing leading up to the first Test in Brisbane.

THE LAST HURRAH   The 1970 Tour Down Under

We arrived in Brisbane on the 27th May and for the first time we felt we could unpack and get a routine going with our training ready for the first Test using our Hotel as a base. The Railway Hotel, what a base what a mess. Ground floor was fully tiled white, like a toilet, that being the reception, bar with a Juke box and toilet. Floorboards and wood staircase up to the lounge area and off this "Lounge" were our bedrooms. First thing the team decided without the managers approval was to carry the Juke box up the very unstable staircase into what was now Our Lounge. The team spirit was building, and for two weeks it was a riot, living with rats in the place but we had some of the most memorable parties, team talks, laughs but in those two weeks our training moved up a few gears, curfews were regular before games but it was usually the last man going to bed as he walked past the jukebox would pick the latest noisiest record to send us all to sleep. Leading up to the first Test we beat Wondai 45 - 7 on the 28th, Queensland 35 - 7 on the 30th all nicely tuned up for Saturday the 6th June for Australia.

In the build up to this much awaited Test we had to withstand plenty of intimidation, personal verbal attacks, press propaganda all to increase the Australian support for their beloved national team. Three weeks in and Johnny Whiteley was proving to be a giant as coach, psychiatrist and tactician with Jack Harding the Headmaster and assassin.

Lang Park, Brisbane 6th June, we arrived in our coach singing Mardigras which was to become our team anthem, Johnny had picked his team with a mix of reputation, form and youth to take on the Aussies. We LOST 37 - 15. The game was physical, Australia were good, the game finishing with an almighty brawl with Cliff Watson having to rescue Dave Chisnall from the attention of the Aussie pack. Headlines next day was Poms lose 1st Test but win the war. Reality check required.

The following day, licking our wounds we travelled to Toowoomba, beat them comfortably. Wednesday, we beat Brisbane and then it was off to Sydney on Thursday the 11th June.

On our arrival in Sydney on the 11th June we were taken to the Olympic Hotel directly opposite the Sydney Cricket Ground, where we would stay until the 6th July in preparation for the remaining 8 matches including the remaining 2 Test matches. The team spirit was building, room sharing was a laugh a minute. Leeds players rooming with Castleford lads, Yorkshire, Lancashire, Wales all sharing stories round the dining room tables, food being served up with an old Bette Davis lookalike, with her thumb in the soup became a feature. Poor old Terry Price was injured at this point with no chance of him playing but he became our ambassador for drinking the Aussies under their own tables but not before he had shown the Australians how to kick goals from well inside his own half.

The rugby we were playing was just getting better by the match. The big tester was playing New South Wales before the second Test on the 20th June. A hard test it was, we drew 17 points apiece. Johnny Whiteley made three changes to the pack and three changes to the backs for the second Test bringing in big Dennis Hartley and Tony Fisher alongside Cliff Watson to face the Aussie front row and brought in a young Jimmy "get some tackling done" Thompson alongside Doug Laughton with Malcolm Reilly last man down. He selected Derick Edwards at full back and brought Syd Hynes and myself in for the right wing pairing.

We beat them with a breathtaking performance 28-7. The lads who didn't play in the Test side played an equal part in this massive team effort, with their support and outstanding performances in a very demanding tour programme. Jack Harding, Johnny Whiteley and Frank Myler our captain were magnificent, handling the civic receptions, the press and the increasing attention, some of it disruptive, in keeping their charges in check and in tune ready for the decider. Our team song Mardigras was never more fitting.

The only concern now was a build-up of injuries particularly to our three full backs who, in defending the Aussie "bombs" rendered them unfit for the third Test on the 4th July. Just two weeks away with four matches to fit in before that date. One of the matches we could only take 16 people on a Dakota aircraft. With its tiny wheel at the back we had to access the plane using a step ladder into the sloping body of the plane. The pilot had his cabin door open all the time giving us instructions and progress on our way. He informed us that the runway (I think it was Wagga airport) at Wagga was not long enough to accept a Dakota aircraft, but the local people had cleared a peanut field for the overrun. He managed the landing on his second attempt kicking up a cloud of dust and peanut residue before we were welcomed by local women with peanut garlands around their necks, as we negotiated the ladder out of the aircraft.

The pilot left the aircraft and came with us to the match, which we just managed to win, and joined us at the after match reception and celebrations. He had to insist we got back to the plane before dark as there was no lights on the runway. A few beers later, a very happy pilot with his 16 passengers landed safely back in Sydney. And so for the final Test. I have never seen people camping outside a stadium the day before any important game, but this game meant so much to the Australian supporters the keenest were not going to miss this one. The cricket ground was full, the crowd were hostile and ready to witness our downfall.

Johnny Whiteley gave the much feared full back roll to Mick Shoebottom. At the first opportunity Australia kicked high towards Mick who took the ball in his stride and made a magnificent clearing run. They kicked again only this time a rampant Dennis Hartley charged down another kick and sprinted under the posts for a try. Despite every effort from the home referee to penalise us and keep Australia in the game, we were magnificent, winning 21-17. We had a game the following day the 5th against Wollongong, and I remember Johnny Whiteley going around doing his best to get a fit team together, with players out of position, players carrying injuries and we still beat them 24-11. We flew from Sydney to Auckland on the 6th July and got settled in the Great Northern Hotel to prepare for three games including the first Test on the 11th July.

Maybe it's the home boy in me but my feelings, straight away in New Zealand, were, this is a bit like home. There did not seem to be the same pressure or intensity towards the job we had arrived to do. The hotels were better for a start and the weather was definitely more like home. We were well received everywhere we went, from eating out Maori style in Rotorua to jet boating up the South Island mountain ranges. Maybe our reputation had preceded us but John was quick to remind us all of the seven matches that faced us in the next three weeks.

At this point I have to remind myself that, and the weather played its part, we did not train a single day whilst we were in NZ. We had to fit in three flights, to Wellington, to Christchurch, back to Auckland for the last Test.

Johnny Whiteley had his work cut out juggling and selecting from a squad of players, a lot who were carrying some sort of injury for the first match at Waikato on the 8th July and then the first Test on the 11th.

We won the first match 42-17 taking us to the first Test at Carlaw Park in Auckland. From the hard baked grounds in Australia to the mud of Carlaw park we ground out a terrific win with 5 tries to 1 and a final score of 19-15. The referees were no different here in NZ trying their best to keep their team in touch with, at times the strangest penalties, like penalising my centre Syd for running into him! We were firing on all cylinders.

Another physical game had now reduced the squad from 26 players to just 19 players for the last five games. We flew to Wellington on the 12th July to beat Wellington in the most atrocious condition 60-8. I can boast to scoring 5 tries that day and winning, for my efforts, a pair of massive mounted Bulls Horns which could not accompany me back to the

THE LAST HURRAH   The 1970 Tour Down Under

airport on our flight to Christchuch. I left them with some adoring fans to decide what to do with them.
The press were now extolling the virtues of our team after this, wet and wonderful win. The rugby we were turning out, was, as per the press, breathless, the likes of which they had never seen before and predicting we could become the first team to have toured Australia and New Zealand and lose only one match. No pressure!

So on to Christchurch to the Embassy Hotel to prepare for the second Test on the 19th we came from behind and won 23-9. From there everyone was taking bets who Johnny would select for the infamous rail trip to Greymouth (a day on, what felt like, the worlds slowest train) This trip is legendary with all touring sides. I was not selected for the journey, I along with other grateful players had the first really relaxing two days until the lads returned from a 57-2 victory played in a thunderstorm.

It was then a flight back to Auckland to the Great Northern hotel where we started, to prepare for the, literally, the Final Test. Carlaw Park again and we were 11-2 down at half time. Two storming tries early in the second half wiped that lead out and then I quote "it was master v pupil highlighted by great individual displays" what a finish we won our final Test 33-16. Game over tour over.

BOAC from Auckland on the 28th July landing Heathrow 29th some journey.

Highlights well where do I start. For me I was privileged to have been part of it. Great players with everything in the mix what rugby, in my opinion, is all about. Ability, speed, strength, vision and add to that respect, resilience, determination and personal pride that team had everything. Place them in the responsible hands of no finer men than gentlemen Jack Harding and Johnny Whiteley, unbeatable. I know we all have the benefit of hindsight but we were there we saw it. It was our "Sporting Life"

From the Railway hotel in Brisbane as a marker for the bonding, we will all have some personal stories and friendships carved out of that trip. I'm sure Johnny Whiteley, who used to baby sit a lot of us on tour with his bedtime stories of all the great players and the memories they have left him with, can recall more than most. A great man.

On that tour we were praised for our off-field work. Players visiting schools to talk about rugby league. Going to school watching youngsters train for rugby league. Crocodile fashion with one individual playing full back and he had to tackle and keep tackling the pupils trying to get past him.

Very impressive.

I recall a comment by Johnny at that time, which was, in 10 years time this lot will be touring and coming over to us and giving us a good hiding! He was 2 years out. 1982 saw the all conquering Australian Kangaroos do just that. We have never recovered.

Just before I finish, I must mention our homecoming. Yes, it was a great feeling being greeted at Manchester airport by our family and friends. My wife couldn't pick me out as we

THE LAST HURRAH   The 1970 Tour Down Under

all walked into arrivals. I had put on one stone in weight on the NZ part of the tour, I know we didn't train but I blamed rooming with Cliff Watson in the Great Northern hotel. We were both regulars at a mobile burger van strategically placed outside the hotel. Quite unique it was. Getting its power plugged into the street lighting. They had a paint brush for the butter and the best pieces of steak hungry boys like me and Cliff, could ever wish for, and they never unplugged their van until Cliff and myself had cleared up.

Three months later, October 1970, Australia came over to play in the World Cup series and, of course the Test team that had been so successful in June and July was, with just the odd exception, the same team. The first match at Headingley was brutal and we beat a refreshed Australia something like 7-2. We both got to the final again at Headingley. If the first was tough this was the hardest game I think anyone has played in or witnessed since but they beat us, just. Was it a game too far. Leeds City Council, I was told, took these two televised games out of circulation as a bad example to younger ones wanting to play rugby league.

I also think what was significant to our game back then, was Roy Francis and his training methods at Leeds. He was years ahead of his time with his attitude to fitness and sprinting. He created the fittest players at Leeds who became almost unbeatable in the late 60s when our game had changed to the four tackle rule. North Sydney poached him from Leeds at the end of 1968 (the water splash final year.) He went over to Australia and he had started to weave his magic there but not in time to reach the national team when we were there. Look at their fitness now, and, do you know who Johnny

Whiteley's mentor was at Hull. Yes. Roy Francis. Food for thought.

It is often felt that players have a tendency to perhaps over estimate what they achieved, how well they played and so on. On this tour it was in all probability the opposite was the case. Journalists are a hard-bitten lot at the best of times having seen so much during their time covering the game. When they offer praise for a particular player or team then you need to listen. When they are praising the opposition then you really do need to listen as it does not happen too often.

The respected New Zealand journalist and rugby league historian from 'The Press' newspaper **John Coffey** when approached to put his thoughts down on paper about the 1970 Tour had this to say:-

JOHN COFFEY
"MYLER'S LIONS DEVOURED THE KIWIS

When I wrote the Kiwis Centenary history in 2007 I considered the 1970 Lions to be the finest touring team to come to New Zealand in my 44 years working at The Press newspaper in Christchurch. Now that traditional tours are sadly, no more, Frank Myler's men will ever retain that status in my estimation.

Coached by the astute Johnny Whiteley, they certainly had the record to prove it. All three Test were won comfortably despite the deceptively close score line in the first. Auckland was beaten convincingly in the traditional tough tour finale, and cricket scores were registered in the other three games. In a champion team two stars sparkled even more brightly- Roger Millward and Malcolm Reilly.

The brilliant Millward crossed for three tries in the first two Tests and ran in a personal treble against Auckland, while Reilly was a multi-skilled colossus packing down at the back of a forward formation which was fronted by such uncompromising characters as Dennis Hartley, Tony Fisher and Cliff Watson.

Great Britain scored 17 tries to New Zealand's four in the three Test matches and truly surged to victory. The Kiwis got within one point during the second half of the 19-15 series opener at Carlaw Park. The home side not only led by nine points but kept its try-line intact during the first half of both the second and third Tests only to succumb by 23-9 at Christchurch and 33-16 back at Carlaw Park.

Though the New Zealand players were still amateurs in 1970, this was an emerging Kiwis combination only starting to suffer from losing players (such as props Bill Noonan and Oscar Danielson) to Sydney clubs. New Zealand had shared the honours in a two-Test home series against the 1969 Kangaroos, but had relied massively on the kicking of full back Don Ladner.

Super boot Ladner supplied 28 points (nine goals and five field goals) of New Zealand's 40 against the Lions, while all of Auckland's points in 23-8 loss came from penalty goals to Ernie Wiggs. Clearly, the Lions defense was as effective in repulsing a Kiwi combination lacking in quality specialist half backs as Millward and Reilly were in creating opportunities to score at the other end of the field.

I like to think the Kiwis learned from their rivals. In 1971 they beat Australia 24-3 at home and won Test series in both Britain and France for a unique Grand Slam. They did so with a Myler-like leader in centre Roy Christian, a dazzling stand-off half in 18 year old Dennis Williams, a rugged front-row of Henry Tatana, Jim Fisher and Doug Gailey and a loose forward, Tony Kriletich, who displayed a Reilly-like work ethic. With Ladner not available the 1971 Kiwis won by scoring tries and overcoming sizeable deficits in two of the Tests."

As Coffey noted the 1970 tourists Reilly (really) were a great team arguably the greatest.

It is somewhat ironic that as the game developed in New Zealand following the Great Britain visit the game here failed to capitalize on the impetus developed by coach Whiteley and his players. Coffey also stated that the Kiwis failed in the same manner to capitalize on the 1971 Kiwis. The reasons in his opinion were, greater interest by Sydney clubs in Kiwi and English players. More importantly the game went over the top with regard to World Cup competitions at the expense of long tours so the opportunity to develop young players was lost.

The Australian leg of the tour was covered by many journalists but one stands out perhaps a little more than others. Ian Heads is a well respected journalist writer and rugby league aficionado and as this tour was going on his career was also coming along as they say. His thought and recollections of that time the Great Britain players spent in Australia are recorded below. He also gave freely of his time to inform the reader of his own recollections of that tour.

Ian Heads

Reflections on a Legendary Tour. (1970) By Ian Heads

Having been somewhere in the vicinity of the game of rugby league at its various levels for much of my life - initially as a watcher in the stand, and then via stumbling upon the unlikely privilege which came my way of being able to gather and share more widely many of the game's stories and great moments as a journalist. I am delighted that Tom Mather within the pages of this book (The Last Hurrah) has chosen to carry the ball further still. He has turned a fresh and searching eye, underpinned by his knowledge and deep passion for the game, onto the events of the stellar season of 1970 when rugby league's champion teams and ancient rivals, Great Britain and Australia, clashed three times in Test matches on colonial soil, constructing in the fury of the battle along the way, a story that endures as one of game's most dramatic of them all.

For the purpose of such an exercise there could be no-one better than Tom to tell the thrilling tale of the events of that bruising season of 1970.

****

Notwithstanding the mists of memory, the arrival in Australia of the champion Great Britain squad of 1970 and all that followed, burn star-bright still in my own mind all these years on, comfortably offering even these 50 years later, clear

THE LAST HURRAH

The 1970 Tour Down Under

recall of a what grew to become as fierce a rugby league Ashes battle as there ever was.

In its thrilling encounters, the contest grew to become one in which a multi-talented GB team ultimately reclaimed the Ashes fair and square with a brilliant late flourish in Game 3 - as 60,000 fans held their collective breath at the Sydney Cricket Ground.

For a variety of reasons, my own sharpness of memory around the events of season 1970 is no great surprise. I had started the previous year as a sportswriter with the Sydney's largest selling morning paper, the Daily Telegraph– understudy there to an outstanding sports journo of his time, Mike Gibson.

Suddenly as the year unfolded, Mike was gone - moving on to the lure of a media opportunity in greener pastures and so it was that I found myself elevated out of Mike's shadow in '69 to cover for the first time as the Tele's senior writer the Sydney Grand Final, churning out on that late afternoon the editor's instruction on my return from the game that day: `Maestro (his nickname for me) "give me 93 pars" – This was no easy task after what had been a tough but stodgy game which volunteered just a single try in its 80 minutes, a game in which outsiders Balmain had out-thought and outplayed favourites South Sydney to steal the prized. Somehow, I fumbled through.

Into 1970 I was given the news that that I would be officially taking over the reins as the Tele's chief RL writer. And so, it was that I found myself tracking the story of the Great Quest of the admirable Great Britain skipper Frank Myler and his men – to win back the Ashes last won on Australian soil in 1962, the tale so graphically told in this book.

Already that year the anticipation had been growing weekly for the arrival of this British side, fuelled by snippets from the UK that found their way into the weekly 'Rugby League News' such as the view of the veteran UK league writer Joe Humphries that the team's 21 year old lock forward Malcolm Reilly was set to make as big an impact in Australia as the legendary Vince Karalius ('The Wild Bull of the Pampas') had on the tour of 1958. This was really saying something, considering the impact the destructive Karalius had had on the Australian forwards back in '58!'

For me the sense of there being something really special in the wind grew in 1970 from my first encounter with the team which would begin their long campaign in Darwin. making their way gradually south from May to July, to Brisbane for the first Test, then south again to the major showdowns, in Sydney. It was apparent from first contact with the GB side of 1970 that this was a particularly well-led bunch, steered impeccably by the impressive trio of Jack Harding (manager), John Whiteley (coach/assistant manager) and Frank Myler, a fine centre and the 31 year old team captain. The players proved to be an amiable, impressive bunch too and in years following I would value the friendships generated back in '70 of the likes of Roger Millward, Malcolm Reilly, Cliff Watson, John Atkinson and others.

Tom Mather captures splendidly in his telling of this story the flavour and the highs and lows of a brilliant tour – one which produced in equal measure great football .and great drama.

In his revisit of the great saga of 1970, Tom rekindles many of my own personal memories of the wildness of the first Test in Brisbane with its fierce exchanges and of the quietness of winning Australian dressing room afterwards and particularly the sight of Aussie prop Jim Morgan dazed and damaged, his legs splayed out. Famously affable Jim had come off second best in a 'Liverpool kiss' exchange with the equally affable Englishman, Cliff Watson.

Australia had won the day - 37-15 but the thought remained strong that afternoon: there was a long way to go in this series. And so there was as the statistics reveal: Great Britain 28-7 (Second Test), GB 21- 17 (Third Test) – with the final lingering image being that of the great 5/8 from Hull, Roger 'the Dodger' Millward scooting away for the clinching try in the deciding Test before an attendance of 61,257, plus a young journo tucked up the back of the SCG Members' Stand.

At that thrilling moment, The Ashes were won and lost. The series had been a cracker.

If you look at the history of the game it is remarkable just how many players went away on tour to Australia and New Zealand as 'good' players but returned to become greats of the game. That hot bed of competition that is a tour made them what they became, sadly that is no longer the case.

Today if a 'good' player wishes to be looked on as a great player then they have to leave the English game and travel down to play in the hot bed that is the NRL. Surely that cannot be right but it is certain that long tours to and from the two countries are a thing consigned to history more's the pity. The Watsons, Reillys, Fishers, Hartleys, Millwards, Hepworths Hardistys and Laughtons, the list goes on and on. Will we ever see their likes again?

PLAYER STATISTICS ON TOUR

Player	games	tries	goals	points
J. Atkinson	18	15	0	45
D. Chisnall	14	1	0	3
R. Dutton	9	2	43	92
D. Edwards	6	0	0	0
T. Fisher	11	2	0	6
P. Flanagan	14	8	1	26
A. Hardisty	16	2	0	6
K. Hepworth	14	4	0	12
C. Hesketh	13	9	0	27
S Hynes	17	19	9	75
B Irving	17	6	0	18
D Laughton	15	9	0	27
P Lowe	15	11	0	33
R. Millward	16	18	23	100
F. Myler	15	3	0	9
T. Price	9	5	51	117
M. Reilly	13	3	0	9
D. Robinson	6	2	1	8
B. Seabourne	8	2	0	6
M. Shoebottom	13	7	0	21
A. Smith	16	15	0	45
C. Sullivan	8	3	0	9
J. Thompson	17	4	0	12
J. Ward	8	0	0	0
C. Watson	13	3	0	9

GAMES PLAYED ON TOUR

GAME 1

22 May   Northern Territories Won 35-12
Played at Richardson Park, Darwin
Attendance 3,000

GAME 2

24 May   North Queensland Won 23-20
Played at Townsville Sports Reserve, Townsville
Attendance 7890

GAME 3

26 May   Central Queensland Won 30-2
Played at Rockhampton Show Ground, Rockhampton.
Attendance 7290

GAME 4

28 May   Wide Bay Won 45-7
Played at Wondai Sports Ground, Gympie
Attendance 3344

GAME 5

30 May   Queensland Won 32-7
Played at Lang Park Brisbane
Attendance 17,071

GAME 6

6 June　　　Australia Lost 37-15
Played at Lang Park Brisbane
Attendance 42,807

GAME 7

7 June　　　Toowoomba Won 37-13
Played at Athletic Oval, Toowoomba
Attendance 6549

GAME 8

10 June　　　Brisbane Won 28-7
Played at Brisbane Exhibition Ground, Brisbane
Attendance 10,117

GAME 9

12 June　　　NSW Drew 17-17
Played at the Sydney Cricket Ground, Sydney
Attendance 31,504

GAME 10

14 June　　　Monaro Won 34-11
Played at Siffert Oval, Queanbeyan
Attendance 9.500

GAME 11

20 June	Australia Won 28-7
Played at the Sydney Cricket Ground, Sydney
Attendance 60,962

GAME 12

21 June	Western District Won 40-11
Played at Bathurst Sports Ground, Bathurst
Attendance 4,400

GAME 13

23 June	Sydney Colts Won 26-7
Played at Endeavour Field, Woolooware
Attendance 14,046

GAME 14

27 June	Newcastle Won 49-16
Played at Newcastle Sports Ground, Newcastle
Attendance 22,655

GAME 15

28 June	Riverina Won 12-11
Played at the Eric Weissel Oval Wagga-Wagga
Attendance 11,000

GAME 16

4 July   Australia Won 21-17
Played at the Sydney Cricket Ground, Sydney
Attendance 61,258

GAME 17

5 July   Southern Division Won 24-11
Played at Wollongong Show Ground, Wollongong
Attendance 7,796

GAME 18

8 July   Northern XIII Won 42-17
Played at Tokoroa Memorial Sports Ground, Tokoroa
Attendance 3,540

GAME 19

11 July   New Zealand Won 19-15
Played at Carlaw Park, Auckland
Attendance 15,948

GAME 20

14 July   Wellington Won 60-8
Played at Basin Reserve, Wellington
Attendance 859

GAME 21

19 July   New Zealand Won 23-9
Played at Orangetheory Stadium, Christchurch
Attendance 8,600

GAME 22

21 July   West Coast Won 57-2
Played at Wingham Park, Greymouth.
Attendance 676

GAME 23

25 July   New Zealand Won 33-16
Played at Carlaw Park, Auckland
Attendance 13,137

GAME 24

27 July   Auckland Won 23-8
Played at Carlaw Park Auckland
Attendance 6,074

POINTS SCORED ON TOUR

Australian Leg of the tour

For Tries scored 97   goals 99   total points 475

Against Tries scored 26   goals 39   total points 196

New Zealand Leg of the tour

For Tries scored 61   goals 37   total points 257

Against Tries scored 9   goals 24   total points 75

Total points for the tour For 732 Against 271

Printed in Great Britain
by Amazon